122 Fun Things To Do In SAN ANTONIO

written by
KAREN FOULK

**INTO FUN, COMPANY
PUBLICATIONS**
A Division of Into Fun, Inc.
Sugar Land, Texas

122 Fun Things To Do In San Antonio
by Karen Foulk

Cover and Map illustrations by Delton Gerdes
Book Layout by Brockton Publishing

Copyright © 1999 Karen Foulk

All rights reserved. No part of this book may be reproduced or transmitted in any form or by any means, electronic, mechanical, photocopying, recording or otherwise, without prior written permission from the publisher.

Library of Congress Catalog Card Number:
98-094071

ISBN 0-9652464-3-4

INTO FUN, INC.
P.O. Box 2494, Sugar Land, Texas 77479
Phone: 281-980-9745   Fax: 281-494-9745

This book contains descriptions including operating times and admission costs of many of the fun and interesting places in the San Antonio area. Although a great deal of effort has gone into making this book as up-to-date and accurate as possible, changes constantly occur. Therefore, before visiting a destination, please call to confirm the information provided herein. Neither Into Fun, Co. Publications, a division of Into Fun, Inc., the owner, nor the author warrant the accuracy of the information in this book which includes but is not limited to price changes, addresses, names, hours of operation, management or conditions of the attraction described.

Dedication

*With all my love,
To my husband, Don,
who thinks I'm having too much fun.*

Michael & Amber

*I want to welcome my new daughter-in-law, Amber,
into our family. She makes a great addition.*

*Rachel
David
Rebecca*

Acknowledgments

Again in appreciation for their contributions,
to the many dear friends, family members,
and associates who make this book possible.

To my husband and children,
for putting up with a busy mom.

To Jerrie Hurd my sister. Read her new book
Lady Pinkerton Gets Her Man.

To Brocky Brown of Brockton Publishing Co.
who makes it all happen.

To Merrill Littlewood, my accountant. He's the best.

To Wendy Nielson, my dedicated Into Fun friend.

To Ken Barrow, for his legal help and advice.

To Annette Hruska, for designing the Into Fun car

To Sharon Cooper, always a friend.

Writing this book was fun. In fact, it's been so much fun, when I call it work my husband laughs.

But this book will make it easy for you. Everything you need to know about San Antonio—for great family adventures—is at your fingertips. Simply choose from the following for fun things to do, terrific places to stay, and delightful places to eat.

San Antonio has wonderful restaurants and I've gone to a lot of trouble to find the best ones. I think you'll enjoy any I've mentioned in the book. Of course, you haven't experienced San Antonio until you've tasted their Tex-Mex cuisine. Plan to eat lots of tasty Mexican food.

The Alamo City has a past; it's one of the oldest cities in the New World, with one of the most popular historical site in Texas—the Alamo. Millions come each year to see the cradle of Texas liberty. The famous courageous trio—Davey Crockett, Colonel William Travis, and James Bowie—are buried in the nearby San Fernando Cathedral. Be sure to see the award-winning IMAX feature **The Alamo, The Price of Freedom** at the Rivercenter Mall.

I loved staying at the Riverwalk Inn. This bed and breakfast, constructed of old log cabins from Tennessee, abounds in charm, with fireplaces in guests' rooms and antique quilts on the beds. After a day of sight-seeing, you're greeted with fresh homemade goodies and lemonade. Believe me, it was tough to leave.

San Antonio is a special place and I can't wait to share this adventure with you. As always, have fun.

Karen Foulk

Table of Contents

What's San Antonio got to Show Off?	9
The Great Outdoors	29
San Antonio's Museums and History	61
San Antonio's Got Culture and Talent	81
Tours and More	99
Amusement Parks & Attractions	113
Where to Eat?	135
Unique Places to Shop	163
Watch for these Annual Events	173
Where to Stay?	181
Golf Courses in the San Antonio Area	195
New Braunfels and the Guadalupe River	203
Index	223

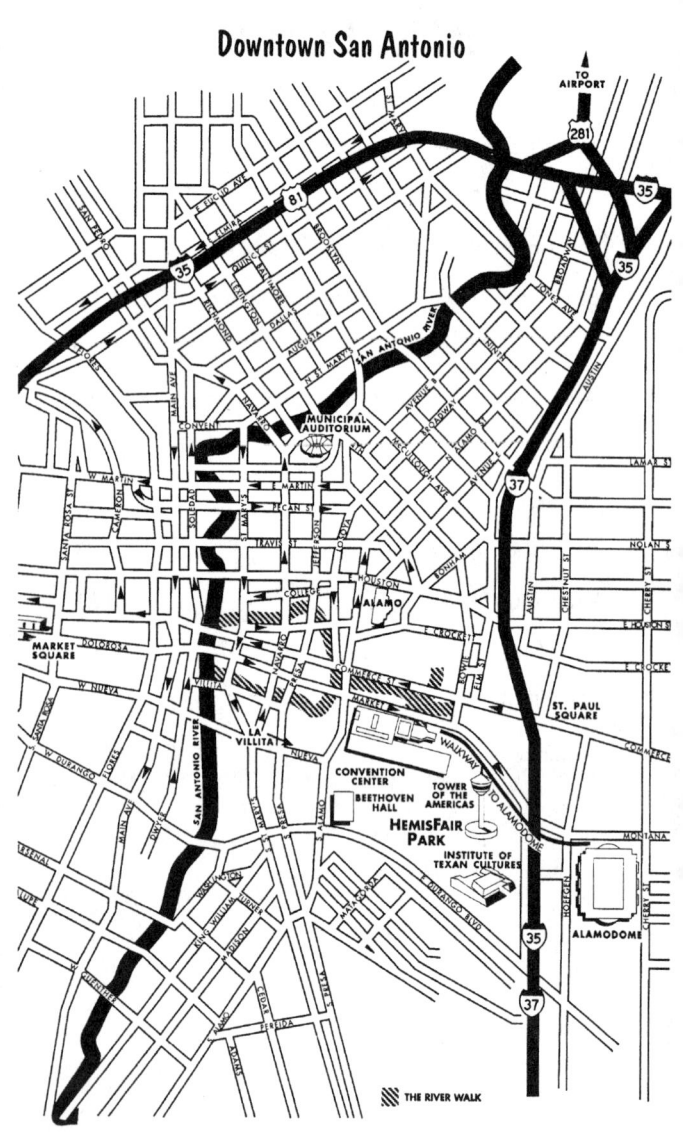

AMTRAK—The Sunset Limited or The Texas Eagle—A fun way to visit San Antonio

Take the **Sunset Limited** to San Antonio. The train runs from Los Angeles, Tucson, San Antonio, New Orleans, Jacksonville, to Orlando. The line includes a stop in Houston, too. Or take the **Texas Eagle**, that runs from Chicago, St. Louis, Little Rock, Dallas, Fort Worth, San Antonio, to Los Angeles. Either line makes an enjoyable way to travel and see Texas. Call 800-USA-Rail (872-7245).

Amtrak offers discounts for any purchaser of *122 Fun Things to do in San Antonio*. Please call 281-980-9745 to find out what savings are available.

AMTRACK "TAKE THE TRAIN"

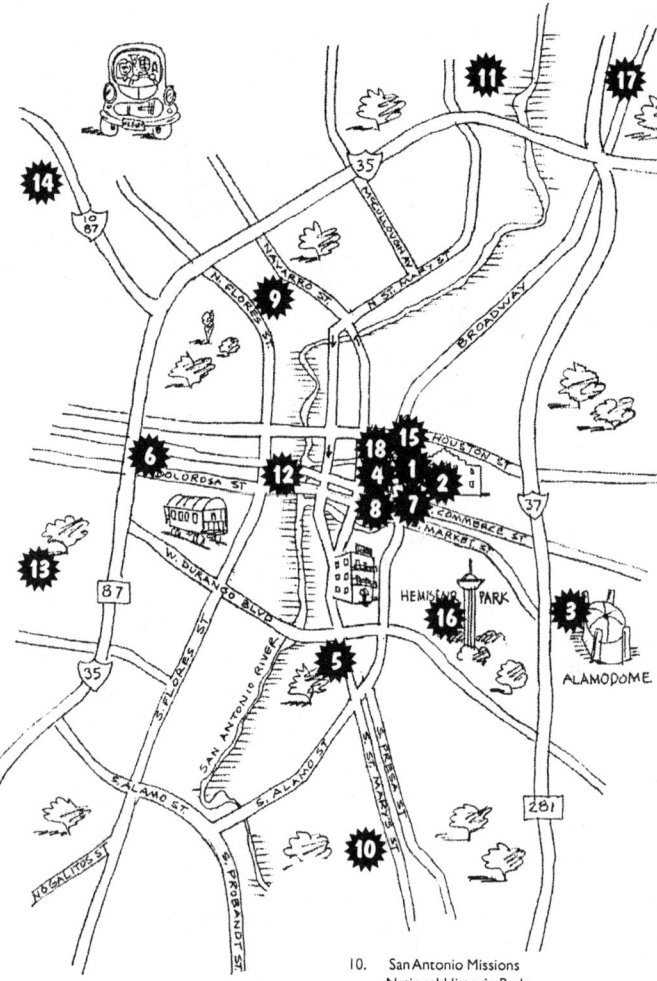

Locations

1. Alamo
2. "Alamo: The Price of Freedom" IMAX Theater
3. Alamodome
4. Ghost Stories of Haunted Places Tours
5. Historic King William District Walking Tour
6. Market Square
7. Rivercenter Mall
8. River Walk Paseo Del Rio
9. San Antonio Central Library
10. San Antonio Missions National Historic Park
11. San Antonio Zoological Garden & Aquariums
12. San Fernando Cathedral
13. Seaworld San Antonio
14. Six Flags Fiesta Texas
15. Texas Adventure Theater
16. Tower of The Americas
17. Witte Museum and the H.E.B. Science Treehouse
18. Yanaguana Cruises

Chapter 1
WHAT'S SAN ANTONIO GOT TO SHOW OFF?

Alamo	10
"Alamo: The Price of Freedom" IMAX Theater	11
Alamodome	12
Ghost Stories of Haunted Places Tours	13
Historic King William District Walking Tour	14
Market Square	15
Rivercenter Mall	16
River Walk Paseo Del Rio	17
San Antonio Central Library	18
San Antonio Missions National Historic Park	19
San Antonio Zoological Garden & Aquariums	20
San Fernando Cathedral	21
Seaworld San Antonio	22
Six Flags Fiesta Texas	23
Texas Adventure Theater	24
Tower of the Americas	25
Witte Museum and the H.E.B. Science Treehouse	26
Yanaguana Cruises	27

What's San Antonio *Got To Show Off?*

ALAMO

300 Alamo Plaza, San Antonio 78205
210-225-1391

San Antonio's birthplace of Texas liberty

"Remember the Alamo" when you visit San Antonio. Our most sacred historical site is one of the state's top visitor draws. Here, on March 6, 1836, Davy Crockett, Colonel William Travis, Jim Bowie, and 186 other men died defending the Alamo. They fought against Mexican General Santa Ana in a battle that bought Texas freedom.

See what remains of this original mission structure. Visit the chapel and Long Barracks Museum, with mementos of the honored fallen men and artifacts from the Republic of Texas. See the letters these famous men wrote to their families before the battle began.

Tour on your own or arrange to go on a tour. Call to schedule a guide. Either way, you must see the Alamo.

The Alamo, established in 1718 as the Mission San Antonio de Valero, forms part of the greatest concentration of Catholic missions in North America. Successfully extending Spain's dominion from Mexico, these missions converted and educated the Native American Indians. The Alamo is now part of the Missions National Historical Park

Hours

(Closed Christmas Eve and Christmas)

Mon. – Sat. . . . . 9 am – 5:30 pm
Sunday . . . . 10 am – 5:30 pm

Cost - Free

Directions - Located in the heart of downtown. From I-10, exit Houston Street, going toward downtown to Alamo Plaza Street and go right.

What's San Antonio Got To Show Off?

"Alamo...The Price of Freedom"
IMAX THEATER
849 E. Commerce #483
San Antonio 78205
210-225-4629
http://www.imax-sa.com

San Antonio's IMAX features the Alamo

San Antonio's IMAX Theater invites you to see an award-winning feature –"The Alamo...The Price of Freedom." With a six-story screen and stereo sound, the IMAX Theater dramatizes the events that took place at the Alamo. Come away with a better understanding and appreciation for what took place. Caution. The feature may be too violent for younger family members. It's realistic, and well done.

Check to see what other interesting shows may be featured. Enjoy a variety of refreshments at the concession stand and visit the unique gift shop with lots of San Antonio memorabilia.

Hours

Daily .... 9 am, 11 am, 1 pm, 2 pm, 4 pm, 6 pm

Cost

Reservation fee	$1.50
Adults	$7.25
Children 3-11 (free if under 3)	$4.75
Seniors 65	$6.75

Directions

Third level of the Rivercenter Mall, downtown around the corner from the Alamo. Located at Commerce and Bowie Streets.

What's San Antonio  *Got To Show Off?*

ALAMODOME

100 Montana Street
San Antonio 78203
210-207-3652

San Antonio's new modern stadium

The Alamodome—painted in bright Southwestern colors with a rectangular, cable-suspended roof—adds wonderful flavor to the existing downtown skyline. One of the most experienced firms in the business designed this fantastic stadium.

Home to the San Antonio Spurs, this $186 million state-of-art facility seats 65,000 people and can host professional events such as football, basketball, and ice skating. Among other things, its permanent ice floor meets the U.S. Olympic Committee's requirements. Take the 45-minute guided tour. See what an impressive place this is.

Conveniently located, you can walk from the River Walk, the Alamo, HemisFair Park, and many downtown hotels. Make this part of your sightseeing in San Antonio.

Hours

Group tours with reservations

Tues. – Sat. . . . . 10 am, 1 pm, 3 pm

Cost

Adults $3
Children 4-12 . . . . $1.50
Children under 4 . . . . Free
Seniors 55+ $1.50

Directions

Located at I-37 between E. Commerce and
E. Durango Streets.

What's San Antonio Got To Show Off?

GHOST STORIES OF HAUNTED PLACES TOURS

Alamo Plaza (in front of the Alamo)
210-436-5417

Go ghost hunting in San Antonio

Tell this to your kids—

"Many believed that the soldiers of the Alamo never received a proper burial. Their souls linger, making San Antonio one of the most haunted cities."

Walk the Alamo City with a "ghost investigator." Tours last 1½ hours. Learn about the most haunted places in San Antonio, where you might have a paranormal experience.

Watch for your guide, a member of the International Ghost Hunters Society. He'll be wearing the black backpack. Make your reservation in advance. Groups of ten or more receive a discount. Call for more details.

Join a special 3-hour "Ghost Hunt" every Saturday night at 10:30 pm. Call for more details. Any teen's idea of fun, right?

Hours

Every night . . . . 8:30 pm

Cost

Adults $10
Children 8 – 17 . . . . $5
Children under 8 . . . . Free

Directions

Meet in front of the Alamo at the defenders' monument, the Cenotaph.

What's San Antonio *Got To Show Off?*

HISTORIC KING WILLIAM DISTRICT WALKING TOUR

A section of town bordering St. Mary's, Washington, Johnson, and Madison Streets
210-224-6163

San Antonio's classic old homes

Well-to-do German families in the mid-1880s built elegant Victorian mansions in what was then a simple frontier town. Today, some of the beautiful old homes are open to the public only on special occasions. Still, a walking tour of this unique and interesting historic district rates high as a favorite to-do in San Antonio.

Get a copy of the self-guided tour from in front of the San Antonio Conservation Society Office at 107 King William Street. Wear comfortable shoes and carry a small jug of ice water when it's hot.

Tour the Steves Homestead, one of the homes that is open to the public. Top this off with a tasty lunch at the Guenther House Restaurant. Browse through the gift shop with delicious baking goods from Pioneer Mills.

Attend the King William Fair's festive activities as a part of the Fiesta San Antonio celebration in April.

Hours
Daily . . . . Until dusk

Cost
Free

Directions
Take St. Mary's Street south of downtown to King William Street.

What's San Antonio Got To Show Off?

MARKET SQUARE

514 W. Commerce, San Antonio 78207
210-207-8600

San Antonio's Mexican Culture

Did you know San Antonio boasts of having the largest Mexican market outside of Mexico? Once a humble farmer's market, it now centers on Mexican culture, with fine restaurants, shops, vendors, mariachi bands, and festivals. Any sightseeing in San Antonio must include Market Square.

One of San Antonio's best restaurants, Mi Tierra opens 24 hours a day. It serves authentic Tex-Mex food made from quality ingredients. Eat here—enjoy tasty breakfasts, lunches, and dinners. See the hand-painted mural on the wall depicting the history of Market Square; stop at the bakery.

The same family that owns Mi Tierra owns and operates La Margarita Mexican Restaurant. This fine restaurant's noisier atmosphere caters to a younger crowd. Open-air patios and strolling mariachis add more pleasure.

Shop at the large indoor center—like those in Mexico. Buy local and imported Mexican goods: jewelry, pottery, Mexican dresses, art, crafts, leather goods, sauces, spices, wrought iron. Newly renovated, the Farmers Market Plaza, once the home of the chili queens, now offers specialty shops and vendors, you won't want to miss. As in Mexico, you can barter for your goods.

Hours

Closed Thanksgiving, Christmas, New Years, and Easter
Summer hours extend until 8 pm

Daily .... 10 am – 6 pm

Directions

The market is at Commerce Street and IH-35.

What's San Antonio Got To Show Off?

RIVERCENTER MALL
101 Bowie Street
San Antonio 78205
210-225-0000

San Antonio's famous shopping mall

What attracts almost as many tourists as the Alamo? The Rivercenter Mall. This beautiful, well-designed shopping mall with three levels overlooks the River Walk. With over a hundred shops—many unique to San Antonio—you can shop 'til you drop. During the hot summer months, the air-conditioned mall makes a nice diversion from outdoor activities. Plan to spend an evening; the mall remains open after most attractions have closed.

Want a lunch or dinner on the go? Eat at the food court. Vendors at the food court serve excellent food.

Hours
Mon. – Sat. . . . . 9 am – 9 pm
Sunday . . . . 9 am – 6 pm

Directions
Located around the corner from the Alamo.
It is on Commerce and Bowie Streets.

What's San Antonio Got To Show Off?

RIVER WALK
PASEO DEL RIO

Winds through the downtown area
210-227-4262

One of San Antonio's major attractions

In 1921, the San Antonio River flooded, killing 50 people and destroying millions of dollars in property. Outraged, folks in San Antonio wanted to do away with the river, covering it over with concrete. Fortunately, the women of the San Antonio Conservation Society saved it from this terrible fate.

Now, when people think of San Antonio, they think of the River Walk. The 2.5-mile section of the river stretches from the Henry B. Gonzales Convention Center on the north to the King William Historic District on the south. In between, sidewalk cafes, specialty boutiques, an outdoor theater, a shopping mall, cruises, art galleries, dining on the water, and quiet places to walk attracts thousands.

Don't miss the Fiesta River Parade in April and the Holiday River Parade in December. Annual events include the Mud Festival, when the river is drained for cleaning; St. Patrick's Day, when they dye the river green, and the Christmas Lighting Ceremony, when thousands of lights decorate the river. What a way to capture the holiday spirit.

Hours

Open 24 hours a day.
Cafes and shops open at 10 am.
Most cafes close at 11 pm.

Directions

Enter the River Walk from most downtown streets; there are over thirty entrances.

What's San Antonio Got To Show Off?

SAN ANTONIO CENTRAL LIBRARY

600 Soledad Street
San Antonio
210-207-2500

Visit San Antonio's new library

You can't miss it. Simply look for the bright "red enchilada" building among the downtown buildings. This state-of-the-art library captures everyone's attention and begs for a visit.

Legorreta Arquitectos, a famous architectural firm from Mexico, used bright colors, natural lights, an atrium, and a mystical sense in the designs. As you walk through the library, observe the subtle colors and the different ways light is brought into the building. The atrium extends from the first floor to the sixth floor, with each floor having its own shape and look. Note the courtyard.

The library's highlights include a large genealogical department, a Latino collection, and a wonderful children's library. Children can enjoy puppet shows and story hours.

Hours

Mon. – Thurs.	9 am – 9 pm
Fri. and Sat.	9 am – 5 pm
Sunday	11 am – 5 pm

Directions

Located downtown at Soledad and Navarro Streets.

What's San Antonio Got To Show Off?

SAN ANTONIO MISSIONS NATIONAL HISTORIC PARK

2202 Roosevelt Avenue, San Antonio 78210
210-534-8833

A National Historic Park within the city limits

Ever wondered how San Antonio got its start? As early as 1690, Franciscan friars established missions in Texas to convert the Indians to Christianity. Beginning with the Alamo, Mission San Antonio de Valero, five of these missions were built along a 12 mile stretch of the San Antonio River. These fortified communities with churches, housing for the Indians, granaries, mills, farmland and ranchland eventually formed the city of San Antonio—the 8th largest in our country.

You can visit these missions as part of a National Historic Park. Catch a tour. The new $9 million visitor center (at the Mission San Jose, 6701 San Jose Drive) features a great video you'll enjoy. It plays every half-hour throughout the day.

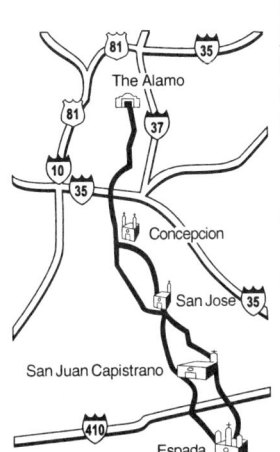

Hours:
Open Daily   9 am – 5 pm

Cost: Free

Map printed Courtesy of San Antonio Convention & Visitors Bureau

What's San Antonio *Got To Show Off?*

SAN ANTONIO ZOOLOGICAL GARDENS & AQUARIUM

3903 North St. Mary's Street, San Antonio 78212
210-734-7183

San Antonio's zoo rates number one

The zoo, nestled inside an old limestone quarry at the headwaters of the San Antonio River, makes a great family outing. Considered one of our country's finest.

Visit the only zoo with endangered whooping cranes. See rare crocodiles and African Warthogs. And don't miss one of the world's largest lizards with the world's deadliest bite—the Komodo dragons from Indonesia. These lizards can kill animals as large as a water buffalo with a single bite.

Offers an exceptional children's zoo that includes an amphibian exhibit, the Conservation Research Center, a petting zoo, a boat ride, and a playground.

Ask about their season passes—they do save. Concessions are available; enjoy browsing in the gift shops. Wear comfortable shoes and plan to take your time.

Hours

Open every day including holidays
Summer hours extend to 8 pm; gate closes at 6 pm.

Daily .... 9 am – 5 pm

Cost

Adults $7
Children 3-11 (under 3 - Free) $5
Seniors 62+ $5

Directions

Go north on North St. Mary's into Brackenridge Park. Follow the signs.

What's San Antonio Got To Show Off?

SAN FERNANDO CATHEDRAL

115 Main Plaza
San Antonio 78205
210-227-1297

San Antonio's famous old cathedral

Visit the oldest cathedral in our country. Named for King Ferdinand III of Spain, who ruled in the 13th century.

At King Phillip V's invitation, fifteen families from the Canary Islands founded the cathedral in 1731 to serve Villa de San Fernando, the original town. The cathedral, after surviving several floods and fires, continues today as a center of religious, community, and cultural events.

James Bowie, one of the important defenders of the Alamo, married here in 1831. See his tomb in the southeast corner of the church. Bowie, Colonel William Travis, and Davy Crockett are buried in the church.

Pope John Paul II visited the cathedral in 1987— a first for Texas. A marble stone marker, inside the church, commemorates the event.

Each year the cathedral performs a Passion Play on Good Friday that reenacts the story of Christ. Attend this special event. Browse in the gift shop with religious items and souvenirs. It opens daily from 9 am – 5 pm.

Hours

Open daily .... 6 am – 7 pm

Cost

Donations are accepted

Directions

The cathedral is on Main Plaza, between Commerce Street and Market Street, in downtown San Antonio.

What's San Antonio   Got To Show Off?

SEAWORLD SAN ANTONIO

10500 Seaworld Drive
San Antonio 78251
210-523-3611

San Antonio has the biggest marine park

Here, deep in heart of Texas, you'll find the world's largest marine park. The park's abundant of marine life includes, of course, the famous killer whales Shamu and Grandbaby Shamu. Experience penguins, sea lions, walruses, beluga whales, otters, and many more animals up close and in a personal way. Pet the dolphins. Watch many of these animals perform amazing stunts in Seaworld's ever-popular shows that will impress the whole family.

Besides having a marine park, SeaWorld San Antonio offers other attractions, including an inverted roller coaster, a children's play area, a water park, several rides and slides. Plan to get wet and spend the day.

Hours
Seasonal

Cost

Adults $31.95
Children 3-11 . . . . $21.95
Children under 3 . . . . Free
Seniors (55+) get a 10% discount

Directions
Located northwest of San Antonio, between 410 West and Loop 1604 on Highway 151.

What's San Antonio Got To Show Off?

SIX FLAGS FIESTA TEXAS

17000 I-10 West
San Antonio 78269
210-697-5050 800-473-4378
www.sixflags.com

San Antonio's new theme park

Want to ride the world's highest and fastest wooden roller coaster? Ride the Rattler the best of roller coasters or ride the Joker's Revenge a roller coaster that goes in reverse. Other highlights include the Gully Washer, a rapid river ride, and a water park. Bring your swim suit and a towel.

This $100 million theme park features Texas' culture and America's past. Enjoy visiting the German, the Mexican, the Old West, and the 1950's Rock N' Roll sections of the park.

Every evening during the summer see a spectacular laser show with fireworks. Very impressive. Stay for the show.

The park offers plenty of food booths, strollers, pet kennels, lockers, foreign currency exchange, and wheelchairs. It is also handicapped accessible.

Hours - Seasonal.

Cost

Person 48" or taller	$33
Person under 48"	$23
Seniors	$23.50
Children under 2	Free

Directions

Six Flags Fiesta Texas is 15 minutes from downtown, at I-10 West and Loop 1604. Take exit 555.

What's San Antonio Got To Show Off?

TEXAS ADVENTURE THEATER

307 Alamo Plaza
San Antonio 78205
210-227-8224

Enjoy this fun attraction

With the help of sophisticated technology, the ghost-like images of Davy Crockett, Colonel William Travis, and James Bowie appear and tell their stories in an attraction similar to ones you find at Disney Land.

As you listen to these men, experience the events of the Alamo for yourself. Appreciate the desire of Texans for freedom.

The hour-long presentation entertains and educates. Your family will enjoy going here. They also have a gift shop and snack bar.

Hours

(Show starts every 30 minutes on the hour and half-hour)
Sun. Thurs. .... 10 am – 5 pm
Fri. – Sat. .... 10 am – 8 pm

Cost

Adults $7.50
Children 3-11 .... $4.50
Seniors $5.90

Directions

Located across from the Alamo.

What's San Antonio Got To Show Off?

TOWER OF THE AMERICAS

600 HemisFair Park
San Antonio 78205
210-207-8615

Get a good look at San Antonio

The Tower of the Americas, constructed for the World's Fair in 1968, stands 750 feet high and offers a spectacular view of the city on any clear day. Take a ride in a glass elevator to a public observation deck. Enjoy the view a little longer; stay for lunch or dinner in the revolving Tower of the Americas Restaurant.

Hours

For observation deck elevators

Sun. – Thurs. . . . . 9 am – 10 pm
Fri. – Sat. . . . . 9 am – 11 pm

Cost

Adults $3
Children 4 - 11 . . . . $1
Children under 4 . . . . free
Seniors 55+ $2

Directions

In HemisFair Park, with the entrance at Alamo Street, between Market and Nueva Streets.

What's San Antonio *Got To Show Off?*

WITTE MUSEUM AND THE H.E.B. SCIENCE TREEHOUSE

3801 Broadway, San Antonio 78209
210-357-1900

San Antonio's adventure museum

Want to learn and have fun at the same time? Go to the Witte Museum. Its newest addition, the H.E.B. Science Treehouse with hands-on exhibits, makes learning fun. Compose music with laser beams, surf the Internet, launch tennis balls, or lift yourself up with pulleys and ropes. Hear native birds of South Texas or see x-rays and medical test results done on an ancient mummy—don't miss this one. And that's not all. With four levels of activities, plan on staying for hours. Entertaining for all ages.

Besides the H.E.B. Science Treehouse, the museum features a fine collection of Texas paintings, ancient Indian cave paintings, dinosaur fossils from Texas, and displays of our state's different ecological areas.

The Witte Museum sits at the edge of Brackenridge Park. The grounds around the museum include three historic homes and native plants that attract butterflies and hummingbirds.

Visit the gift shops. Overnight camping for youth can be arranged. Group rates are available.

Hours & Costs

Open until 6 pm in the summer. Closed Thanksgiving, Christmas Eve & Day

Mon., Wed., Sat.	10 am – 5 pm
Tuesday	10 am – 9 pm
Adults	$5.95
Children 4–11 (under 4 are free)	$3.95
Seniors	$4.95
Tuesday 3 pm – 9 pm	Free

Directions - North of downtown on Broadway.

What's San Antonio Got To Show Off?

YANAGUANA CRUISES

315 E. Commerce
San Antonio 78205
210-244-5700

Cruise the San Antonio River

Yanaguana means "clear or refreshing", the Indian name for the San Antonio River. Enjoy a 40-minute guided narrative cruise along the River Walk. Learn about its history and interesting points. Cruises leave every ½ hour, depending on the season.

Use the water taxi service to go along River Walk. With 9 different stops, conveniently get from major hotels such as the Sheraton, the Adam's Mark, the Marriott and the Landing to where ever you need to go. Rides cost $3.25. For $10, get a day pass, or for $25, a 3-day pass.

Dine aboard one of the cruises. Make reservations for a candlelight dinner cruise with some of the restaurants featured on the River Walk.

Hours
Open holidays

Daily .... 9 am – 10 pm

Cost
for narrative tour

Adults $5.25
Children under 5 .... $1
Seniors $3.65

Directions

Ticket stations: Rivercenter, across from the Hilton Palacio del Rio and the Holiday Inn River Walk.

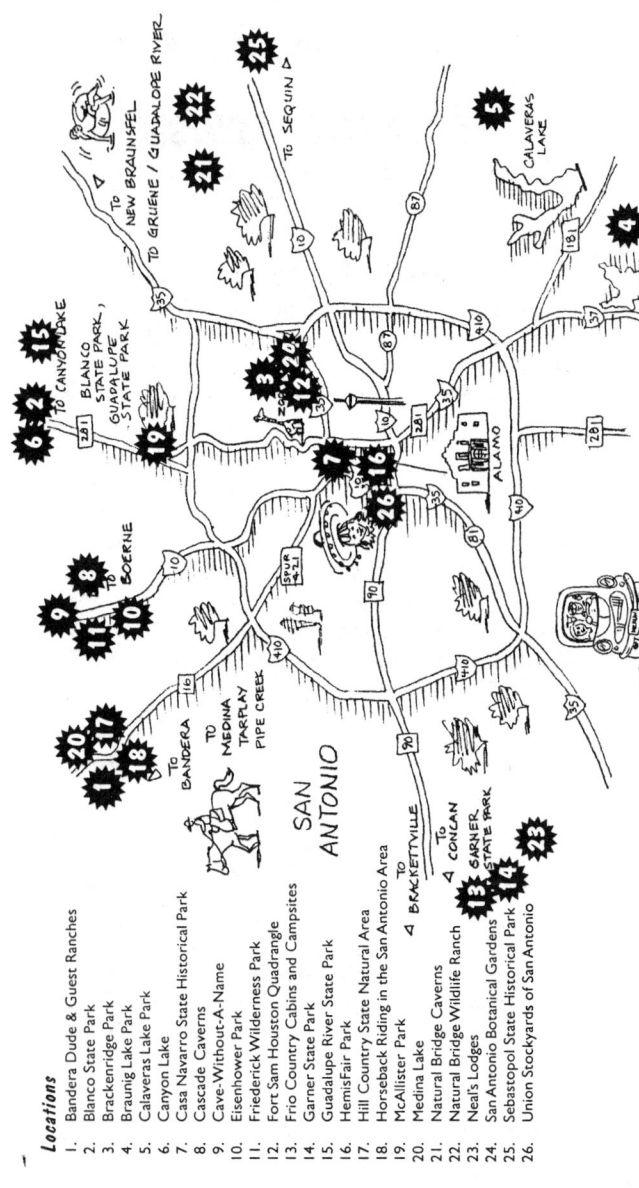

Locations

1. Bandera Dude & Guest Ranches
2. Blanco State Park
3. Brackenridge Park
4. Braunig Lake Park
5. Calaveras Lake Park
6. Canyon Lake
7. Casa Navarro State Historical Park
8. Cascade Caverns
9. Cave-Without-A-Name
10. Eisenhower Park
11. Friederick Wilderness Park
12. Fort Sam Houston Quadrangle
13. Frio Country Cabins and Campsites
14. Garner State Park
15. Guadalupe River State Park
16. HemisFair Park
17. Hill Country State Natural Area
18. Horseback Riding in the San Antonio Area
19. McAllister Park
20. Medina Lake
21. Natural Bridge Caverns
22. Natural Bridge Wildlife Ranch
23. Neal's Lodges
24. San Antonio Botanical Gardens
25. Sebastopol State Historical Park
26. Union Stockyards of San Antonio

Chapter 2
THE GREAT OUTDOORS
Nature, Caves, Parks, Dude Ranches, Zoos

Bandera Dude and Guest Ranches	30
Blanco State Park	34
Brackenridge Park	35
Braunig Lake Park	36
Calaveras Lake Park	37
Canyon Lake	38
Casa Navarro State Historical Park	39
Cascade Caverns	40
Cave-Without-A-Name	41
Eisenhower Park	42
Friederick Wilderness Park	43
Fort Sam Houston Quadrangle	44
Frio Country Cabins and Campsites	45
Garner State Park	46
Guadalupe River State Park	47
HemisFair Park	48
Hill Country State Natural Area	49
Horseback Riding in the San Antonio Area	50
McAllister Park	52
Medina Lake	53
Natural Bridge Caverns	54
Natural Bridge Wildlife Ranch	55
Neal's Lodges	56
San Antonio Botanical Gardens	57
Sebastopol State Historical Park	58
Union Stockyards of San Antonio	59

The Great Outdoors

BANDERA DUDE AND GUEST RANCHES

The "Cowboy Capital of the World" in San Antonio's backyard

ABUNDARE RIVER RANCH

HCI, Box 433; Bandera 78003
830-796-4076

Stay at this 600-acre guest ranch on the Medina River. The ranch offers guests tennis, a pool, a playground, and a gift shop. Sleep in plantation-style accommodations.

Directions - 4 miles southeast of Bandera. Take 173 to Bottle Springs Road and go 2.5 miles.

BALD EAGLE RANCH

P.O. Box 1177; Bandera 78003
830-460-3012
www.baldeagleranch.com

Want an escape? This ranch caters to an adult clientele with personalized service.

Directions - 11 miles from Bandera on 1077, next to the Hill Country State Natural Area.

CHUKKA CREEK GUEST RANCH

Rt. 1, Box 801; Bandera 78003
830-460-7859

Stay at a ranch that offers trail rides, cattle drives, and cottages with kitchenettes.

Directions - 5 miles west of Bandera on FM 470.

The Great Outdoors

DIXIE DUDE RANCH
P.O. Box 548; Bandera 78003
830-796-44 • 800-375-9255
www.tourtexas.com/dixieduderanch

Bandera's oldest dude ranch. Guests stay in cabins or in the lodge. The ranch features horseshoes, a heated pool, a playground, basketball and volleyball. Activities include cowboy breakfasts, bonfires, cookouts, hayrides, western entertainment and more. See the old historic barn and cemetery on the premises.

Directions - 9 miles from Bandera on FM 1077.

FLYING L GUEST RANCH
P.O. Box 1959; Bandera 78003
800-292-5134 • 830-460-3001
www.flyingl.com www.flyingl.com

At this ranch, suites come with microwave, refrigerator, and cable TV. Take a trail ride along San Julian Creek or go fishing, hiking, and swimming. The ranch has an 18-hole golf course and driving range, also tennis and basketball courts. Children will enjoy the petting corral and playground. Night activities include dancing, campfires, sing-alongs, trick roping, and more. Meals are served buffet style.

Directions - 1 mile from Bandera, South on Hwy 173.

THE YELLOW ROSE RANCH
HC-2, Box 176; Tarpley 78883
830-562-3456

Stay in one of the ranch's two large guesthouses. The ranch offers scenic horseback riding through the Hill Country.

Directions - 22 miles NW of Bandera on FM 470.

LH7 RANCH RESORT

P.O. Box 1474; Bandera 78003 • 830-796-4314

You choose. Accommodations at this ranch include 10 native stone cottages with kitchenettes, 10 RV sites or camping. Activities include hiking, hayrides, nature walks, and bird watching. Be sure to take the ranch tour. See Texas longhorn cattle and enjoy fishing in the lake.

Directions - 5 miles NW of Bandera on FM 3240.

LIGHTNING RANCH

Rt.1, Box 1015; Pipe Creek 78063 • 830-535-4096

The Lightning Ranch's activities include horseback riding, barbecues, hayrides, swimming. Sleep in comfortable cottages.

Directions - .33 miles from Highway 16 on 1283.

MAYAN RANCH

P.O. Box 577; Bandera 78003 • 830-796-3312

With lots to offer, this 324-acre spread runs along the Medina River. You will enjoy swimming, tubing, fishing, hayrides, horseback riding, tennis, pool, and volleyball. Activities also include Texas barbecues, steak cookouts, cowboy breakfasts. For accommodations, stay in one of the cottages or the lodge.

Directions - .5 mi. NW of Bandera on 6th & Pecan.

TWIN ELM GUEST RANCH

P.O. Box 117; Bandera 78003
888-567-3049 • 830-796-3628

Take your choice. This ranch accommodates guests with cabins or bunkhouses. Guests enjoy horseback riding, rodeos, hiking, river swimming, hayrides, fossil hunting, and other fun activities.

Directions - 3 miles NW of Bandera on FM 47.

The Great  *Outdoors*

RUNNING R RANCH
Rt. 1, Box 590; Bandera 78003
830-796-3984
www.rrranch.com

Want to go on a picnic? Guests can request a tasty picnic lunch. The cabin accommodations include 3 meals and horseback riding.

Directions - 9 miles west of Bandera on RR 1077, next to the Hill Country State Natural Area.

SILVER SPUR DUDE RANCH
P.O. Box 1657; Bandera 78003
830-796-3037
www.texasusa.com/ranches/silvspur.html

This ranch's ideal location makes it attractive. Bordering the Hill Country State Natural Area, it offers scenic horseback rides and guest accommodations with home-style cooking. Eat cowboy breakfasts and Texas barbecues. Facilities includes a pool table, a game room, and a playground.

Directions - 10 miles south of Bandera on FM 1077.

THE FARM COUNTRY CLUB
P.O. Box 831; Bandera 78003
830-589-2276

Need a group outing? This ranch caters to group excursions with plenty of activities: barbecues, western bands, trick ropers, hayrides, gunfighters, rodeos, horseshoe pitching, swimming, and more.

Directions - 8 miles from Bandera on FM 2828.

The Great Outdoors

BLANCO STATE PARK

P.O. Box 493
Blanco 78606
830-833-4333
512-389-8900 for reservations

Hill Country camping

Camp where early explorers and settlers camped. Besides camping, the 100-acre park offers swimming, picnicking, hiking, wildlife observing, boating, and fishing. You will enjoy fishing for perch, catfish, bass, and winter rainbow trout. Be sure to hike the beautiful ¾-mile trail. Self-guided maps of the trail are available at the park store. Ask about the guided hiking tour.

The park provides restrooms with showers, campsites with water and electricity, and day-use facilities.

Hours

Open 24 hours a day

Cost

Day use fee for adults (13 and older) $3
Campsites .... $12 - 14

Directions

Located in Blanco, 40 miles north of San Antonio. Take U.S. Highway 281 to Park Road 23, four blocks south of the town.

The Great  *Outdoors*

BRACKENRIDGE PARK

3910 N. St. Mary's Street
San Antonio 78212
210-736-9534

Spend a day at Brackenridge Park

Brackenridge Park's wonderful attractions make it one of the most desirable year-round family destinations in San Antonio. Entertain your family with an endless number of things to do. Featuring one of the ten top zoos in the U.S., this 400-acre scenic park doesn't stop here. Be sure to see the ever-popular Witte Museum with its H.E.B Science Treehouse and the newly renovated Japanese Tea Garden. Other activities include riding horses at the Brackenridge Stables and taking a scenic train ride through the trees on the Brackenridge Eagle Miniature Train. The kids will find the Kiddie Park and the Skyride are lots of fun.

Each of these attractions has its own operating schedule and admission fee except for the Japanese Tea Garden, which is free.

The family will love having cookouts along the river. Rent paddleboats or go canoeing. The park also has a public golf course and driving range.

Hours (for attractions)

Mon. – Fri. . . . . 9:30 am – 5 pm
Sat. – Sun . . . . .9:30 am – 5:30 pm

Cost

Call ticket office for admission prices.

Directions

Located 2 miles north of downtown San Antonio. The main entrance is at the 2800 block of Broadway.

The Great Outdoors

BRAUNIG LAKE PARK

17500 Donop Road
San Antonio 78232
210-635-8289

San Antonio's fishing hole

Maintained by the San Antonio River Authority. You'll enjoy fishing here with your family. Feed by a tributary of the San Antonio River, the lake is known for trophy-size bass. Catch catfish, crappie, shad, bluegill, and red drum. Facilities include fishing guide and boat rental services.

Camping and picnicking are also available. You'll find bird watching opportunities: white-winged dove, cactus wren and black-throated sparrow.

Hours

Summer
Open 24 hours a day
Winter
Daily .... 6 am – 6 pm

Cost

Adults $3
Children (ages 7 – 16) $1
Children (under 6) .... Free

Directions

Located 15 miles southeast of downtown San Antonio. Take S.H. 37 south, exit 130 (Donop Road) and follow the signs.

The Great **Outdoors**

CALAVERAS LAKE PARK

12991 Bernhardt Road
Devine 78112-0181
210-635-8359

Enjoy San Antonio's outdoor activities

The lake offers excellent year-round fishing opportunities: bass, catfish, crappie, shad, bluegill, and red drum. Operated by the City of San Antonio, the 146-acre park includes camping, picnicking, canoeing, boating, and wildlife observing.

You'll enjoy seeing interesting birds: golden-fronted woodpeckers, cactus wrens, long-billed thrashers, white-winged doves, and long-billed thrashers.

Hours

Open 24 hours a day

Cost

Adults	$3
Children 7-16	$1
Children under 6	Free

Directions

Located 15 miles southeast of San Antonio. From downtown, take 37/281 south and exit U.S. Hwy. 181 south. Turn left on Loop 1604. Go two miles, then turn left on Stuart Road. Go .5 mile to the entrance.

The Great Outdoors

CANYON LAKE

U.S. Army Corps of Engineers, Fort Worth Division
HC4, Box 400, New Braunfels 78133-4112
830-964-3341

One of the most scenic lakes in Texas

Situated in steep hills, Canyon Lake's average depth of 43 feet offers excellent opportunities for water sports, birding, picnicking, camping, and hiking. The Upper Guadalupe River makes available some of best white water kayaking and canoeing in Texas. Below the dam, the river's mild current is a haven for tubers.

Spend the day at one of Canyon Lake's many parks. Located along the shoreline, these parks feature a variety of facilities for day users and campers: Comal Park, Canyon Park, Potter's Creek Park, Overlook Park, Crane's Mill Park, Jacob's Park, and North Park. Some of these parks provide extras such as boat ramps, marines, and convenience stores.

Hours

Day use parks
Summer hours extend until 9 pm

Daily . . . . 7 am – 7 pm

Camping parks

Daily . . . . 7 am – 10 pm

Cost

Day use parks

Adults $1
Max. Per car $3
Camping . . . . $6 - $16

Directions

Canyon Lake is 20 miles north of New Braunfels. Take S. H. 46 and FM 2722 north, or 306 north of I-35.

The Great ✦ *Outdoors*

CASA NAVARRO STATE HISTORICAL PARK

228 S. Laredo Street
San Antonio
210-226-4801

An interesting historical site

Don Jose Antonio Navarro, born in 1795, contributed much to the state of Texas. He not only ranched, but as a popular statesman, he signed The Texas' Declaration of Independence. He also participated in the convention that brought Texas into the Union. He attended as the only native Texan.

Thanks to the San Antonio Conservation Society, you'll enjoy touring his home. Built in 1848, the house gives visitors a good example of early Texas architecture and furnishings. Exhibits inside the home make early Texas history interesting.

Plan to take the personalized guided tour and take your time.

Hours

Closed Mondays and Tuesdays
Wed. – Sun. 10 am – 4 pm

Cost

Adults $2
Children 6 – 12 . . . . $1
Children under 6 . . . . Free

Directions

In downtown San Antonio on the corner of South Laredo and West Nueva Streets. Use West Nueva.

The Great Outdoors

CASCADE CAVERNS

Cascade Cavern Road, Boerne 78015
830-755-8080

Oldest operating cave in Texas

These caverns date back millions of years. Over time single droplets of water have created what we see today—magnificent formations. See evidence of Indians using the upper caverns for ceremonies and hear stories of an old German hermit who lived in its entrance. Designated as a historical site, the caverns will excite any family looking for a good time.

As you descend 190 feet below the surface, you will see beautiful living formations. Best of all, the tour ends with a grand finale—a 100-foot waterfall. Tours take about 45 minutes. Rubber-soled shoes are a must. The cave is not accessible to strollers and wheelchairs. Bring your camera.

Enjoy the picnic area with barbecue pits and a 105-acre RV park with a swimming pool.

Hours

Summer

Daily	9 am – 6 pm

Winter

Mon. – Fri.	10 am – 5 pm
Sat. – Sun.	9 am – 5 pm

Cost

Adults	$8.50
Children ages 3-11	$5.50
Children under 2	$1

Directions

Take I-10 West from San Antonio 16 miles. Exit Cascade Caverns Road and follow the signs.

The Great Outdoors

CAVE-WITHOUT-A-NAME
325 Kreutzberg Road, Boerne 78006
830-537-4212

One of the most beautiful caverns in Texas

What would you call these caverns? Over 60 years ago, a contest to name the cave was held. A young boy wrote that he thought it was too pretty to name. Out of hundreds of entries, the owner liked his best. In the '70s, attempts were again made to rename the cave, but the name remains the same today.

Visit one of the largest caves in Texas. See huge underground rooms with beautiful live limestone formations that continue to grow. Rubber-shoed shoes are a must as you wander along the gravel paths and down the concrete stairs that take you over 100 feet below the surface. The tour lasts approximately 1 hour and 15 minutes. Cameras are allowed. It is privately owned and not as well known as other Hill Country caverns. Call ahead before going.

Hours
(Closed weekdays during the winter)
Six days a week (Closed Tues.). 9 am – 5 pm

Cost
Adults $7
Children 5 – 11 . . . . $4
Children under 5 . . . . Free

Directions
Located 40 miles northwest of San Antonio. Take I-10 west and exit Hwy 87 which becomes Main Street and follow into Boerne. Continue thru Boerne to the 4th light. Turn right onto 474 and go 6 miles to Kreutzberg Road. Follow signs 5.5 miles to the cave.

The Great Outdoors

EISENHOWER PARK
19399 N.W. Military Highway
San Antonio 78257
210-207-3066 • 210-698-1057

Go hiking at this city park

San Antonio's Eisenhower Park features hiking trails. You'll find 5 miles of well-marked hiking trails; some are even wheelchair accessible. The observation tower lets you view San Antonio's skyline on a clear day. The park also features primitive camping, picnicking, and wildlife observing. The kids will enjoy the playground.

The park borders an old rock quarry and is near the Friedrich Wilderness Park.

Hours
Daily ....6 am until dusk

Cost
Free

Directions
Located in northwest San Antonio next to Camp Bullis. From I-10, take Camp Bullis Road to FM 1535.

The Great 🐎 *Outdoors*

FRIEDRICH WILDERNESS PARK

21480 Milsa, San Antonio 78256
210-698-1057

A popular place for enjoying the great outdoors

Get out the hiking boots. Friedrich Wilderness Park provides an easy escape from the hectic urban life of San Antonio. Located in forested hills, the park makes available opportunities for hiking, picnicking, and birding.

Hikers get a choice in hiking trails. Take an easy one like the Upland Range Trail or experience more of a challenge on trails like the Vista Loop and the Main Loop Trails. All trails are well marked with map boards. Folks in wheelchairs will enjoy the Forest Ranger Trail. Arrange for a guided interpretive hike with a park naturalist. Call for details.

You'll find an abundance of wildlife: white-tailed deer, cottontail rabbits, squirrels, and raccoons. As a favorite spot for birding, the park offers a chance to see rare species of birds like the golden-cheeked warbler and the black-capped vireo. Other birds such as the northern orioles, painted bunting, northern bobwhites, and greater roadrunners frequent the area.

Depending on the weather and time of year, the park tends to be crowded. Best times to beat the crowds are on weekdays or during the summer and winter months.

April-September *(Tues. – Sun. only)*   8 am – 8 pm
October-March *(Tues. – Sun. only)*   8 am – 5 pm

Cost - Free

Directions - In northwest San Antonio. Take I-10 West to the Camp Bullis Road Exit. Turn left and go on the underpass, then right on the access road. Go 1 mile and turn left on Oak Drive. Follow to a T intersection and go right on Milsa.

The Great Outdoors

FORT SAM HOUSTON QUADRANGLE

Building 123 S4 Road, Ft. Sam Houston
San Antonio 78234
210-221-1151

Fort Sam Houston's rich in history

Fort Sam Houston's rich history dates back to 1845, when Texas joined the Union and the U.S. Army moved to Texas. After building a permanent fort in 1870, the army constructed the quadrangle, with its famous brick clock tower, as a supply depot.

Popular with folks, the fort makes the quadrangle available to the public. The quadrangle houses many tame animals: white-tailed deer, chickens, rabbits, squirrels, geese, ducks, and peafowl. According to legend, these animals descended from those brought here by Geronimo. He lived in the quadrangle for a while as prisoner with other Apache warriors.

In 1898, Theodore Roosevelt's Rough Riders stopped at the quadrangle for supplies on their way to Cuba. They camped in an area now known as Roosevelt Park.

Today the headquarters for the 5th U.S. Army resides at Fort Sam Houston. While on base, enjoy these two museums: the Ft. Sam Houston Museum and the U.S. Army Medical Museum.

Hours

Mon. – Fri. . . . . 8 am – 6 pm
Sat. and Sun. . . . . Noon – 6 pm

Cost

Free

Directions

At Fort Sam Houston, the corner of Grayson St. and New Braunfels Ave. Take Broadway north to Grayson St. and go right.

The Great Outdoors

FRIO COUNTRY CABINS AND CAMPSITES

P.O. Box 188
Concan 78838
830-232-6625

Exciting family retreat

A great place if you want to get away for a weekend. You'll find 60 air-conditioned cabins plus campsites located on the cool, clear Frio River. Inner tubing at its finest. Most who stay here make reservations to return before leaving.

Offers a country store with picnic supplies. Float trips are available. Over 30 campsites with electricity and water, 10 campsites for tent camping.

Seasonal

Open from May through September. July is the peak season. Frio Country takes reservations anytime.

During the peak season, a three-night stay is required.

Cost

Cabin prices are based on four people;
prices start at $55 a night.

Directions

Located approximately 80 miles west of San Antonio on the Frio River. From San Antonio, take Highway 90 west to Sabinal. Turn right on Highway 127/187 at the only red light. Go through the city of Sabinal (in about 2 miles the highway separates). Take Highway 127, about 20 miles. Just before Highway 127 ends and hits Highway 83, turn right on River Road. Frio Country Store and office is 2 miles on River Road, on the left.

The Great Outdoors

GARNER STATE PARK
HCR #70 Box 599, Concan 78838
830-232-6132 • 512-389-8900 for reservations

The most visited park in Texas

Named after John Nance Garner, a former U.S. Vice President, Garner State Park opened in 1941. The park developed and improved with the help of the Civilian Conservation Corp.

Situated in the beautiful Hill Country. The clear, rock-bottomed Frio River flows through the park, creating all kinds of recreational opportunities and attracting lots of guests for many reasons. The park features camping, hiking, nature study, picnicking, boating, fishing, swimming, and biking. And during the summer, enjoy dancing every evening, playing miniature golf, and tubing on the river.

The park's campsites provide water; some also have electricity. Rent paddleboats and inner tubes. The park facilities also include screened shelters, picnic tables, and a dining hall. Stay in one of the 17 cabins built by the CCC.

Office hours

Daily .... 8 am – 5 pm

Cost

Entrance fee (overnight campers) 13+ $3
Entrance fee (day use per person) 13+ $5
Campsites w/water .... $10 -$12
Campsites w/water and electricity . $15 -$17
Shelters .... $20 -$22
Cabins .... $55 -$60

Directions

Located 8 miles north of Concan on the Frio River. Take U.S. Highway 83, turn east on FM 1050 and go .5 mile to Park Road 29, follow to the entrance.

The Great Outdoors

GUADALUPE RIVER STATE PARK

3350 Park Road 31
Spring Branch 78070
830-438-2656
512-389-8900 for reservations

Enjoy tubing the Guadalupe River

Make your reservations well in advance. The 1938-acre park tends to be busy in the summertime and on holidays. People love to go tubing on the Guadalupe River and the park provides an ideal place to camp along the river. You'll also enjoy the rugged beauty of this scenic park.

Other activities include fishing, swimming, canoeing, picnicking, wildlife observing, and hiking. See armadillos, white-tailed deer, squirrels, raccoons, and a variety of birds.

Hours

Open year round

Daily .... 8 am – 10 pm

Cost

Day use per person 13+ $4
Camping $12-15

Directions

Located 30 miles north of San Antonio. Go 8 miles west of junction U.S. Highway 281 and U.S. Highway 46 to Park Road 31, then 3 miles to the entrance.

The Great Outdoors

HEMISFAIR PARK
200 South Alamo
San Antonio 78205
210-207-8572

Visit the park with the tower

San Antonio celebrated its 200th birthday with the 1968 World's Fair. The site of the World's Fair, HemisFair Park, still hosts attractions you'll want to include in your sightseeing trips.

See The Water Park's 12 acres of fountains, wading pools, and landscaping that make the park a pleasant place to stroll. Be sure to take the elevators to the observation deck of the Tower of the Americas and lunch in the revolving restaurant.

The Downtown All-Around Playground built by volunteers will entertain any child for hours. The playground features a wood-constructed play area with a space tunnel and castle.

Best of all visit the Institute of Texan Cultures, a museum about the different cultural influences in San Antonio and South Texas.

Hours
Open 24 hours a day

Directions
The entrance is on Alamo Street between Market and Nueva Streets.

The Great Outdoors

HILL COUNTRY STATE NATURAL AREA

Route 1, Box 601, FM 1077, Bandera 78003
830-796-4413 • 512-389-8900 for reservations

Scenic trails for hiking and riding

The only state park that allows horseback riding. This rugged 5000-acre park features miles of trails for horseback riding, hiking, mountain biking, primitive camping, and backpacking. Numerous ranches in the area provide horses and trail rides. Trails for riding or hiking range from easy to difficult. Some have wonderful scenic views.

Swim in the spring-fed creek or plan to go fishing. Sections of the area are available for off-road cyclists. You'll delight in the wildlife: white-tailed deer, lizards, red-tailed hawks, and more.

The park offers no amenities such as potable water, paved roads, or restrooms. Plan to bring your own supplies. Overnight camping is not allowed on Monday nights. Call the information hotline, 800-792-1112, before going, especially during hunting season.

Hours

Spring, Summer and Fall

Thurs. – Mon. . . . . 8 am – 10 pm

Winter

Camping and hiking is allowed from noon on Fridays until 10 pm on Sundays

Cost

Day use fee (over 13) . . . . $3 each
Day use fee (under 13) . . . . $2 each

Directions

45 miles NW of San Antonio. Hwy 16 to Bandera. South on Hwy 173 one mile, then FM 1077 for 10 mi.

The Great 🐎 *Outdoors*

HORSEBACK RIDING IN THE SAN ANTONIO AREA

Here are ways to enjoy horseback riding

Rent a horse from the following outfits. Horses rent by the hour. Some offer half-day and full-day rides and will include meals. Contact the following for more details.

CHUKKA CREEK
830-460-7859
Half- and full-day rides. Mornings include breakfast. See Texas Longhorn cattle and an abundant of wildlife.

DESERT HEARTS COWGIRL CLUB
830-796-7446
Features 2-hour rides in the Hill Country.

GRAND MEADOWS
830-796-3738
Riding lessons for both English and Western styles.

LOMA DE BLANCA
830-741-4596
Horseback riding, camping, and lodging with meals.

LOST WIND LIVERY
830-796-7292
Rent a horse by the hour. Must be at least 8 years old.

LH7 LONGHORN OUTFITTERS
830-796-4314
Scenic rides. Longhorn cattle.

LIGHTING RANCH
830-535-4096 • 800-668-4096
Horseback riding for 2 hr, half-day, or full-day.

The Great Outdoors

RUNNING R RANCH
830-796-3984
Scenic rides on ranch with guides.
Must be at least 6 years old.

SILVER SPUR DUDE RANCH
830-796-3037
Horseback riding on scenic ranch.

TWIN ELM GUEST RANCH
830-796-3628
Morning rides on hilltop with view; afternoon rides along the river.

WAGON WHEEL STABLES
830-966-2153
Offers guided trail rides. All riders welcome.

THE YELLOW ROSE
830-562-3456
Offers a variety of rides and lessons.
Ponies for children.

The Great Outdoors

McALLISTER PARK
13102 Jones Maltsberger Road
Wetmore 78247-4221
210-496-9001

Visit this unique park

McAllister Park's wooded 856 acres is located in the suburbs near the San Antonio airport. Maintained by the City of San Antonio, the park features picnicking, fishing, camping, and birding. It includes 7 miles of biking and hiking trails with a section that's wheelchair accessible.

In the spring and summer, you will enjoy seeing numerous shoreline birds.

Hours
Daily .... 6 am – 10 pm

Cost
Free

Directions

From 410 Loop, exit on 281 and go 3 miles to Bitters Road. Turn east on Bitters Road then take Starcrest to Jones-Maltberger Road. Go left 1 mile to park entrance.

The Great Outdoors

MEDINA LAKE
Scenic lake in the Hill Country

The 5575-acre Medina Lake situated in the hills and limestone bluffs provides excellent fishing for yellow catfish. Plan to spend the day catching varieties of bass, catfish, crappie, and shad. You will enjoy the lake's amenities: camping, boating, picnicking, and water sports. Medina Lake is a favorite for divers.

Hours
Daily .... Dawn to dusk

Cost
Free

Directions
Located 30 miles west San Antonio on FM 1283. Enter the park on Park Road 37.

The Great Outdoors

NATURAL BRIDGE CAVERNS

26495 Natural Bridge Caverns Road
Natural Bridge Caverns 78266
210-651-6101

Visit the largest underground caverns in Texas

Water still drips from the ceiling of the old caverns as the massive, colorful formations continue to grow. Hear underground water gushing overhead. See underground rooms the size of football fields.

In 1960, ranchers allowed four college students to explore the cave. Surprised, the men discovered a 60-foot passageway that lead to huge underground cavern systems. The caverns were opened to the public in 1964.

You'll find the guided narrative tour fascinating. Wear cool comfortable clothing. The caverns remain at 70 degrees year-round, but with humidity over 90%, the temperature feels much warmer. The tour takes 1.5 hours. Athletic shoes or shoes with rubber soles are a must. Strollers are allowed, but there are two narrow stairways.

Hours

Summer hours extend to 6 pm

Daily .... 9 am – 4 pm

Cost

Adults $9
Children 4 – 12 .... $6
Children under 4 .... Free
Seniors 65+ $8

Directions

From San Antonio, take IH 35 north to exit #175 (Natural Bridge Caverns Road) 3009 and go east 8 miles.

The Great Outdoors

NATURAL BRIDGE WILDLIFE RANCH

26515 Natural Bridge Caverns Road
Natural Bridges Caverns 78266
830-438-7400
www.nbwildliferanchtx.com

See exotic animals from your car

Your admission fee will include a bag of feed for the animals. (And the animals know that.) That's what's fun about the Natural Bridge Wildlife Ranch. Be prepared as you drive into the park; eager animals will swarm your car in anticipation of a handout. It's the ostriches and the llamas, however, that provide the greatest thrill. If you survive, stop in at the gift shop for your "I survived the ostriches" tee shirt.

The wildlife park features animals from all over the world. Animals roam the open ranchland, allowing visitors to view them in a natural setting.

Take the kids to the petting zoo and to see the other caged animals. Be sure to visit the gift shop for souvenirs of your adventure. Your kids will be love this one.

Hours

Daily (til 6:30 pm - Summer) .... 9 am – 5 pm

Cost

Adults $7.50
Children 3-11 .... $5
Children under 3 .... Free
Seniors 65+ $6.75

Directions

From San Antonio, take IH 35 north to exit #175 (Natural Bridge Caverns Road) 3009 and go east 8 miles.

The Great Outdoors

NEAL'S LODGES

P.O. Box 165 (Hwy 127)
Concan 78838
830-232-6118

A favorite family vacation spot

One of the best-kept secrets in Texas. Located on the beautiful Frio River in the heart of the Hill Country. Rent one of their 66 cabins. Choose from rustic cabins that are favorites of many to ones that are more lavish.

Offers RV hookups, camping facilities near the river, a country store, a restaurant, a washateria, a video game room, hayrides, horseback riding, innertube rentals, and much more.

Reservations are taken as early as January 1 for the entire year. A deposit and a three-night stay are required in the summer.

Summer Season

Memorial Day through Labor Day

Cost

Cabins per night	$39 - $150
Per person hayrides	$5
Horse rides	$12.50
Float trips	$2
Innertubes	$3
Campsites	$14.50
RV Hookups	$16.50

Directions

Located 80 miles west of San Antonio in the town of Concan, go 23 miles north of Uvalde on Highway 127.

The Great Outdoors

SAN ANTONIO BOTANICAL GARDENS

555 Funston Place, San Antonio 78209
210-207-3250

Considered one of the finest

Lush describes the gardens. Whether you like roses or wildflowers, you'll delight in what you'll see here. The botanical gardens portray many different native Texas landscapes and other interesting vistas. The Biblical Garden shows off plants referred to in the Bible such as fig trees and date palms. The blind will enjoy the Touch and Scent Garden—everyone else will, too. With interpretive signs in Braille, the garden yields plants interesting to our other senses. And for the kids visit the especially designed Children's Garden.

The award-winning, $6.5 million Lucile Halsell Conservatory Complex contains 90,000 square feet of climate-controlled space. Explore the tropical house, the desert house, the palm house, the fern house, and much more.

The San Antonio Conservation Society's efforts preserved the 1896 Carriage House that now houses the gift shop and tearoom.

Hours

Closed Christmas & New Year's

Daily .... 8 am – 5 pm

Cost

Adults $4
Children 3-13 (under 3 Free) $1
Senior 55+ $2

Directions

Five minutes from downtown. Take Broadway north to Funston and go right. Entrance will be on the left.

The Great Outdoors

SEBASTOPOL STATE HISTORICAL PARK

704 Zorn Street, Sequin 78155
830-379-4833

See this unique old house

In a vista of 300-year-old live oaks and antique roses, this old pioneer home, built in 1856, is one of the finest examples of early Greek Revival architecture. The State of Texas recognizes the house as a Registered Texas Historic Landmark and it lists with the National Register of Places.

The limecrete construction gives the house special notice. Only a few such houses with this unusual and unique construction still remain. Let your personal tour guide explain how they were built.

See the original furnishings on the upper level of the home. You'll find it interesting to learn about the Zorn family — who owned and maintained the home for generations. As a turn-of-the-century mayor, Joseph Zorn loved innovations. His progressive thinking resulted in a power plant on the Guadalupe River, which brought electricity to the small town of Sequin.

Hours

Saturdays and Sundays ..... 9 am – 4 pm

Cost

Adults $2
Students $1
Children under 5 .... Free

Directions

30 minutes from San Antonio. Take I-10 to S.H. 46 south one mile and turn left onto Court Street. The park will be one mile on your left.

The Great Outdoors

UNION STOCKYARDS OF SAN ANTONIO

1716 S. San Marcos Street
San Antonio 78207
210-223-6331

Visit these famous old stockyards

In early frontier days, farmers marketed their agricultural goods in San Antonio. After the Civil War, cattle drivers on their way to northern markets stopped here for their supplies.

With the arrival of the railroad, the cattle business changed. Ranchers then sold their cattle to buyers who shipped them to markets by rail. In 1889 a group of ranchers formed the San Antonio Stockyards Company to meet the demands of the cattle industry. Today, these 100-year-old stockyards continue as a major trading center for livestock.

You'll get a thrill watching real working cowboys at the oldest stockyard west of the Mississippi. Public auctions continue every Monday and Wednesday morning. Visitors are welcome.

Hours

Mondays and Wednesdays . . . Begins at 9 am

Cost

Free

Directions

From I-10, take S.H. 35 North, exit San Marcos and follow to the stockyards.

Locations

1. Air Force History and Traditions Museum
2. Buckhorn Saloon and Museum
3. Espada Aqueduct and Acequia
4. Fort Sam Houston Museum
5. Hanger 9 / Edward H. White Museum
6. Hertzberg Circus Museum
7. Institute of Texans Cultures
8. La Villita Historic District
9. Mexican Cultural Institute
10. McNay Art Museum
11. Pioneer Trail Drivers and Texas Ranger Memorial Museum
12. San Antonio's Children's Museum
13. San Antonio Museum of Art
14. Spanish Governor's House
15. Steves Homestead
16. Texas Transportation Museum
17. U.S. Army Medical Museum
18. Yturri-Edmunds Museum

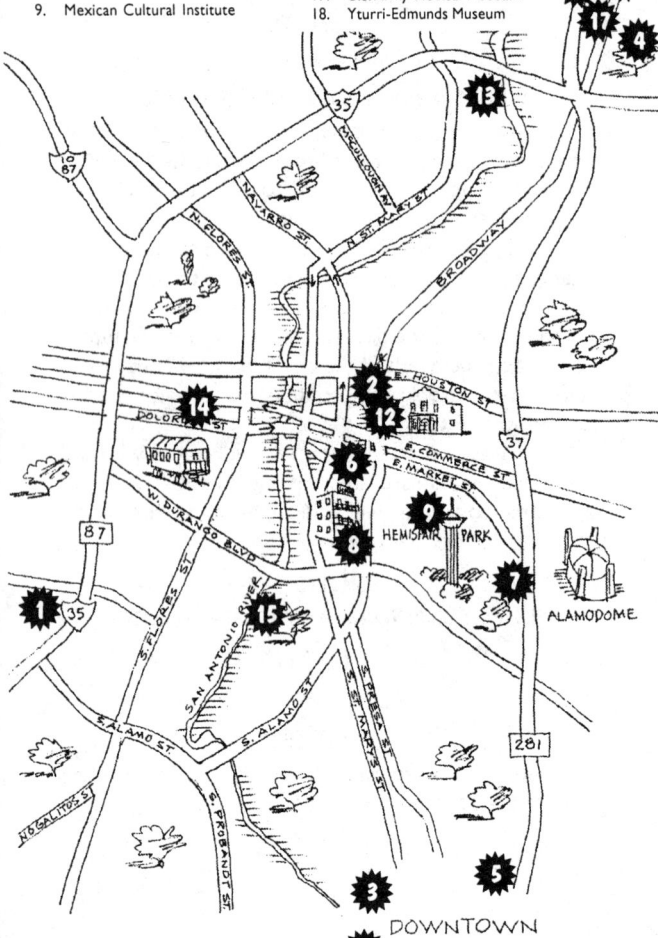

DOWNTOWN SAN ANTONIO

Chapter 3
SAN ANTONIO'S MUSEUMS AND HISTORY

Air Force History and Traditions Museum 62
Buckhorn Saloon and Museum 63
Espada Aqueduct and Acequia 64
Fort Sam Houston Museum..................... 65
Hanger 9 / Edward H. White Museum 66
Hertzberg Circus Museum...................... 67
Institute of Texans Cultures..................... 68
La Villita Historic District 69
Mexican Cultural Institute 70
McNay Art Museum 71
Pioneer, Trail Drivers
    and Texas Ranger Memorial Museum 72
San Antonio's Children's Museum 73
San Antonio Museum of Art.................... 74
Spanish Governor's Palace..................... 75
Steves Homestead 76
Texas Transportation Museum.................. 77
U.S. Army Medical Department Museum 78
Yturri-Edmunds Historic Site 79

Museums And History

AIR FORCE HISTORY AND TRADITIONS MUSEUM

Building 5206
Lackland Air Force Base
210-671-3055

See a military aviation museum

Focusing on our military aviation history, the museum's collection includes rare aircraft and aircraft components from World War I to the present. See engines, weapons, and memorabilia housed inside the museum and a static display of aircraft outside on base grounds. The display of aircraft features World War II, Vietnam, and other aircraft, including an SR-71 Blackbird.

Enjoy the variety of military aviation videos the museum's theater has to offer. The museum also has a library.

Hours
Closed federal holidays
Mon. – Fri. .... 8 am – 4:30 pm

Cost
Free

Directions

From Military Drive to the Luke entrance.
Go left on Jary and follow it around to Orville Wright Drive. Take a right. Building 5206 will be straight ahead.

Museums   And History

BUCKHORN SALOON AND MUSEUM

318 E. Houston Street, San Antonio 78205
210-270-9400 • 210-270-9469

See rare and exotic collections of wildlife

In 1881, trappers and cowboys exchanged deer antlers for a drink in Albert Friedrich's saloon. Numerous antlers now hang on the saloon's walls. Today, the collections also include the Hall of Horns, the Hall of Feathers, and the Hall of Fins—taxidermy examples of exotic and native wildlife—with numerous dioramas and exhibits. The Hall of Horns is considered to be the world's largest collection of antlers.

The museum affords visitors the opportunities to see animals that are rare or extinct like, Passenger Pigeons and the Irish elk antlers. The wax museum, the Hall of Texas History features life-size figures of heroes and other influential people from 1532 – 1898.

Enjoy seeing the Lone Star Buckhorn Museum at its new downtown location. Take a guided tour or tour on your own. Tour ends with a complimentary beer or root beer.

Hours

Daily . . . . 10 am – 6 pm

Cost

Adults $9.99
Children (6 - 12) $7.95
Children under 5 . . . . Free
Seniors $7.95

Directions

Downtown at Houston and Navarro Streets.

Museums And History

ESPADA ACEQUIA AND AQUEDUCT

9044 Espada
210-229-5701
www.nps.gov/saan/

See a 250-year-old irrigation system

In the 1700's, Spanish missionaries and Indians constructed five dams, seven gravity-flow ditches, and an aqueduct—a 15-mile network of irrigation ditches—to carry water to their fields. The watering system resembles ones found in Spain, built by the Moslems. The system supplied water for almost 3500 acres of farmland.

Many of the canals no longer exist. Examples of the acequia can be found around San Antonio: at the Alamo, in HemisFair Park, and at the Yturri-Edmunds Historic Site.

Take a drive south of downtown on the Mission Trail to the Espada Dam. See where the water empties into the acequia madre—the mother of all ditches—and then the Espada Aqueduct, one of the oldest arched Spanish aqueducts in the United States. It is still used by area farmers to water crops.

Continue on south to Mission Espada. See some of the best remaining examples of the acequia. You'll find San Antonio's early means of irrigation interesting.

Hours
Open 24 hours a day

Cost
Free

Directions

Take S. St. Mary's, south of downtown, to the Mission Trail, beginning on Mission Road. Follow the signs. Obtain a map from any of the Missions.

Museums And History

FORT SAM HOUSTON MUSEUM NATIONAL HISTORIC LANDMARK

Building 123, 1210 Stanley Road
Fort Sam Houston 78234
210-221-1886

Discover Fort Sam Houston

Any history buff's dream. The museum focuses on the history of the U.S. Army, from its arrival in 1845, when Texas joined the union, to our present day. See weapons from flintlock rifles to automatic machineguns, old photographs, helmets, uniforms and much more.

Enjoy seeing documentary war videos that continue to play throughout the day. Videos last approximately 30 minutes to an hour, depending on the feature. The museum also offers literature on the fort's history. Obtain handouts on the Quadrangle, Geronimo, and other interesting things about Fort Sam Houston.

Outside see a static display of artillery pieces. Ask for more details.

Hours

Closed Mondays, Tuesdays, and federal holidays
Wed. – Sun. . . . . 10 am – 4 pm

Cost
Free

Directions
Located on Stanley Road, Building 123.

Museums And History

HANGER 9/ EDWARD H. WHITE MUSEUM

Brooks Air Force Base
Building 671
210-536-2203 • 210-531-9767 reservations

Museum on flight medicine history

Housed in the Air Force's oldest aircraft hanger, the museum focuses on the history of flight medicine. The museum features a section on flight nurses, early flight instrumentation, test pilots and more.

Brooks Air Force Base developed the food and pressure suits used by astronauts for the space industry.

Hours
Mon. – Fri. . . . . 8 am – 4 pm

Cost
Free

Directions
S.E. Military Dr. and IH-35

Museums And History

HERTZBERG CIRCUS MUSEUM

210 W. Market Street, San Antonio 78205
210-207-7819 • 210-207-7810 Recording

See historical circus memorabilia

Unusual describes the Hertzberg Circus Museum. See items like Tom Thumb's carriage, his violin, and his rifle. Learn about some interesting circus performers. Ever hear of a three-legged man? How about the world's tallest man or fattest woman? Your kids will find this museum fascinating.

Begin with the interesting 30-minute video, then explore the displays. The museum houses a priceless collection of artifacts, over 20,000 circus-related items.

One Saturday a month, the museum invites families to participate in activities: magic shows, juggling acts, mime performances, and mask-making workshops. Call or watch the local newspaper for upcoming events. The museum also makes computers available to children with software the kids will enjoy.

Park the car across the street in the River Bend Parking Garage. The parking garage offers one hour of free parking for museum attendees.

Hours

Mon. – Sat. . . . . 10 am – 5 pm
Sunday (Summer only) . . . . 1 pm - 5 pm

Cost

Adults $2.50
Children (3 – 12) $1
Children under 3 . . . . Free
Seniors $2

Group rates are available

Directions

At the corner of S. Presa and Market.

Museums   And History

INSTITUTE OF TEXAN CULTURES
801 South Bowie Street, San Antonio 78205
210-458-2300
210-458-2291 group reservations

Texas folk culture comes alive at this museum

People from many countries settled the great state of Texas. In fact, some 27 different ethnic groups have influenced the present-day culture. Learn more about Texas history and what these people contributed. The museum features a dome show, "Faces and Places of Texas," with a multimedia exhibit of 36 screens. Plan on an hour and forty minutes to see the show.

Part of the University of Texas, the museum was built for the 1968 HemisFair. Docents will explain interesting aspects of exhibits: for example, how cowboys on a cattle drive cooked on the open range. Take a guided tour of the museum with your family. The museum also provides two hours of free parking with admission.

Hours
Closed Mondays, Thanksgiving, and Christmas
Tues.– Sun. .... 9 am – 5 pm

Cost
Adults $4
Children (2-12) $2
Seniors 65+ $2
Group rates $2

Directions
Located in HemisFair Park, on Bowie and Durango Streets. Enter on Durango.

Museums And History

LA VILLITA HISTORIC DISTRICT
418 Villita Street, San Antonio 78205
210-207-8610

Visit the shops and plazas, keeping its history in mind

The La Villita Historic District is distinctive in San Antonio's rich history. Known as "San Antonio's Little Village," it originated as one of the first Spanish settlements along the San Antonio River. At La Villita, Santa Ana prepared for the famous battle against the 189 defenders of the Alamo.

The once-humble dwellings of this old Spanish settlement now serve as unique little shops. You will find arts and crafts of all kinds.

In April, La Villita comes alive with the 10-day Fiesta celebration, *A Night in Old San Antonio*. Considered the largest historic preservation festival in the country, the event is a fundraiser for the San Antonio Conservation Society. For the event, La Villita splits into areas of different ethnic foods and music, providing a taste of San Antonio's culture and history. You'll want to participate in this well-organized and popular event.

Hours
Closed Thanksgiving, Christmas, and New Year's Eve
Daily . . . . 10 am – 5 pm

Cost
Free

Directions
Across from the entrance to HemisFair Park near the River Walk. On S. Alamo and Nueva Street.

Museums And History

MEXICAN CULTURAL INSTITUTE
600 HemisFair Park, San Antonio 78205
210-227-0123 • 210-224-8633

Visit the Aztec building in HemisFair Park

San Antonio's Mexican Institute brings Mexican culture to its own doorstep. The Mexican institute promotes close historical, cultural, social, and traditional ties with Mexico. Inviting Mexico's artists and performers to San Antonio, the institute offers cultural experiences open to the public.

The institute offers conferences, performing arts, a movie series, visual arts, and workshops. With these activities, the institute hopes to create a better understanding of the language, literature, history, art, customs, and folklore.

Experience for yourself what this institute has to offer. See the art gallery with visiting artists' works on display. Impressive. Ask for a schedule of their upcoming events.

Hours
Closed Mondays

Tues. – Fri. .... 10am – 5pm
Saturday and Sunday .... 10am – 5pm

Cost
Free

Directions
In HemisFair Park. Use the entrance on Alamo Street.

Museums   *And History*

McNAY ART MUSEUM

6000 N. New Braunfels, San Antonio 78209
210-824-5368
www.mcnayart.org

San Antonio's classical art museum

Marion Koogler McNay left her beautiful Mediterranean-style home, the surrounding property, her art collection, and part of her wealth to establish this art museum. Opening in 1954 as the first modern art museum in Texas, the museum displays a wonderful art collection. You'll delight in works of the 19th and 20th century great masters: O'Keefe, Van Gogh, Matisse, Picasso, Cezanne, Pollack, Gauguin, and Toulouse-Lautrec.

Stroll the lush landscaped gardens with water fountains, a Japanese garden, fishponds, garden sculptures, and a courtyard. Bring along a picnic lunch.

Be sure to watch for upcoming events and visiting exhibits. The museum hosts works of artists you won't want to miss.

Hours
Closed Thanksgiving, Christmas, and New Year's Eve
Closed Mondays

Tues. – Sat. . . . . 10 am – 5 pm
Sun. . . . . Noon – 5 pm

Cost
(Donations accepted)
Free

Directions

Located at the corner of North New Braunfels Avenue and Austin Highway. Take Broadway north of downtown to Austin Highway.

Museums   And History

PIONEER, TRAIL DRIVERS AND TEXAS RANGER MEMORIAL MUSEUM

3805 Broadway, San Antonio 78209
210-822-9011

Honors the Texas Rangers and early pioneers

Stephen F. Austin needed to protect the 300 families he brought here to settle the Texas frontier. Hiring ten men to roam the range and provide protection, he created the first law enforcement agency in North America. Even today, the Texas Rangers make up the strongest law enforcement group in Texas.

See old photographs of famous Texas Rangers hanging on the walls in this fine old museum. Dedicated to the legacy, this museum lets us relive their day. See guns, saddles, and the badges of the legendary men.

The museum also honors the trail drivers who drove some 10,000,000 head of longhorn cattle to markets in the north between 1866 and 1895. See saddles, branding irons, spurs, and barbed wire carried on the trail.

Take note of the building that houses this museum. The rotunda is a miniature replica of the one at the state capitol building in Austin.

Hours

Closed Thanksgiving, Christmas, and New Year's Eve

Summer Daily . . . . 10 am – 5 pm
Winter Daily . . . . 11 am – 4 pm

Cost

Adults $2
Children (4 – 12) (under 4 Free) . . . . $.50
Seniors (55+) $1.50

Directions - Next to the Witte Museum.

Museums   And History

SAN ANTONIO'S CHILDREN'S MUSEUM

305 E. Houston Street, San Antonio 78205
210-212-4453

San Antonio's fantastic children's museum

With hands-on exhibits geared for children ages 2-10, the museum will fascinate your kids for hours—parents too. It offers over 80 educational and interesting things to do.

Set up as a miniature San Antonio, the exhibits focus on everyday life such as shopping, going to the doctor, banking, gardening, and constructing buildings and streets. Climb the replica of the H.E.B Science Treehouse or even take a pretend trolley ride around town.

Other fun activities involve recycling, nature, art, and even bubble blowing. A favorite of many is the Teddy Bear Hospital, with opportunities to help teddy bear patients get well.

Family friendly, the museum offers excellent annual memberships that make the museum affordable for everyone. Enjoy one hour of free parking at the Mid-City Garage.

Hours & Costs

Monday	9 am – noon
Tues. – Friday	9 am – 5 pm
Saturday	9 am – 6 pm
Sunday	Noon – 4 pm
Per person	$4
Members & Children under 2	Free
Annual family membership	$50

Directions - One block from the River Walk on Houston and Navarro Streets.

Museums   And History

SAN ANTONIO MUSEUM OF ART

200 W. Jones Avenue, San Antonio
210-978-8100 • 210-829-7262
www.samuseum.org

See the restored old Lone Star Brewery

The largest brewery in Texas at the turn of the century sat vacant for decades until its potential was realized and the building was restored. You'll find this renovated old brewery fascinating. It now houses one of the finest collections of art in the State of Texas and is listed in the National Register of Historic Places.

Ask for a guided tour or visit the museum on your own. You'll enjoy highlights that include Mexican folk art, a Pre-Columbian gallery, Asian art, and ancient art of the antiquities. See paintings of the 1800's, Chinese art, and much more.

New to the museum is the Nelson A. Rockfeller Center for Latin American Art. Be sure to include this in your visit. Stop into the gift shop with art books, jewelry, crafts, and other artistic items. Coming here is a must. The museum is free to the public on Tuesdays from 3 pm – 9 pm.

Hours & Costs

Closed Thanksgiving and Christmas • Closed Mondays

Tuesday	10 am – 9 pm
Wed. – Sat	10 am – 5 pm
Sunday	Noon – 5 pm
Adults	$4
Children (4 – 11)	$1.75
Members & Children under 3	Free
Seniors 65+	$2

Directions - Go North on Broadway to W. Jones St. Go left. Will be on the right.

Museums And History

SPANISH GOVERNOR'S PALACE

105 Plaza De Armas, San Antonio 78205
210-224-0601

One of the oldest structures in San Antonio

The Spanish Governor's Palace meant domination in the New World. The early Spanish stronghold helped to discourage French ambitions and established a Spanish ruling government. Built for the aristocratic class, many a dignitary stayed here.

Today, the Spanish Governor's Palace opens its doors for a unique experience in early frontier living. Built in 1749, it was luxurious and elegant for its day. You'll find the house restored to its original state, filled with authentic furnishings. Its well-built walls are three-feet thick. Notice the carvings on the front door, depicting the story of Spanish American history. As a registered National Historic Landmark, I'm sure you will find the house interesting.

Hours

Mon. – Sat. . . . . 9 am – 5 pm
Sunday . . . . 10 am – 5 pm

Cost

Adults $1
Children (7 – 13) . . . . $.50
Children under 7 . . . . Free
Seniors $1

Directions

Located between Commerce and Dolorosa Streets, behind city hall.

Museums And History

STEVES HOMESTEAD

509 King William Street, San Antonio 78204
210-225-5924

Tour home in the Historic King William District

Edward Steves made his fortune operating the local lumber mill. With that fortune, he built a magnificent 3-story house along the San Antonio River in the most prominent part of town. Built in 1876 and restored to its original beauty, the house reflects an interesting era in San Antonio's history.

Out back, the Steves estate includes the River House, the first indoor swimming pool in San Antonio. See the 2-story carriage house, built with a storage room and servant's quarters.

If you love history and old mansions, you'll find the guided tour intriguing. Include the 1-hour tour of this historic home with the self-guided walking tour of the King William Historic District. Maps of the historic district are available at the San Antonio Conservation Society at 107 King William.

Hours

Daily .... 10 am – 4:15 pm

Cost

Adults $2
Children under 12 .... Free

Directions

Located in the Historic King William District at St. Mary's and King William Streets.

Museums And History

TEXAS TRANSPORTATION MUSEUM

11731 Wetmore Road, San Antonio 78247
210-490-3554

A haven for any train enthusiasts

Focusing on means of surface travel, the 5000-square-foot Texas Transportation Museum makes for a great family outing.

See the fine collection of antique horse-drawn carriages. The museum's unique collections include a horse-drawn fire truck, a Studebaker Carriage, a doctor's carriage, and a Victorian Brougham Carriage.

Inside the museum you will find an old restored train depot from Congress, Texas. Walk though the old steam locomotive, the business car, and the Pullman car you'll find on display. The museum features three working model railroads and an array of classic cars.

"All aboard!" Best of all take a ride on a real standard-gauge train. The museum offers train rides out back on a 1/3-mile track for any guest on the first Sunday of every month, every 45-minutes between 12:30 pm and 3:30 pm. Rides are free with the admission price, but donations will be accepted.

Hours

Thurs. Sat. and Sun. . . . . 9 am – 4 pm

Cost

Adults $4
Children under 12 . . . . $2

Directions

Located near the airport. Take 281 north from downtown. Go east on 410. Exit Wetmore Road and go north past the airport.

Museums And History

U.S ARMY MEDICAL DEPARTMENT MUSEUM

Building 4011
2310 Stanley Road (Building 1046)
Fort Sam Houston 78234
210-221-6358 • 210-226-0265
210-221-6277 group reservations
www.phoenix.nev~ameddmus

Museum on the U.S. Army Medical History

Home of the U.S. Medical Department, the museum focuses on the U.S. Army medical history from the Revolutionary War to Desert Storm. See a collection of Army medical equipment and vehicles including two ambulances from World War II.

You'll enjoy the photographs and displays. Exhibits feature some of the healing practices used by the Army during war and peace. See uniforms and even makeshift medical equipment.

Hours
Closed Mondays and federal holidays
Tues. – Sun. . . . . 10 am – 4 pm

Cost
Free

Directions
Fort Sam Houston is located at the corner of
Harry Wurzbach and Stanley Road.
Ask at the gate for detailed directions.

Museums And History

YTURRI-EDMUNDS HISTORIC SITE

128 Mission Road, San Antonio 78210
210-534-8237

Over 250 years ago, the Spanish missions gave sections of their farmland to Indian tenants. As one of these land grants, the Yturri-Edmunds Historic Site allows us a look at early times in Texas.

Today, the property consists of an 1860's adobe house. Ownership of the house continued in the same family for over a hundred years, until 1961.

See an original 1820's mill, restored in 1972. Running from beneath the house to the mill is a remnant of the old Spanish irrigation system—the acequia.

Two more structures saved by the San Antonio Conservation Society have been move to this site, the 1881 Oge Carriage House and the 1855 Postert House.

Hours
Thurs. – Sat. . . . . 10 am – 4 pm

Cost
Adults $2
Children under 12 . . . . Free

Directions
From downtown take S. St. Mary's going south to Mission Road. Turn right and follow Mission Road as it curves to the left. Will be on the corner of Mission and Yellowstone Roads.

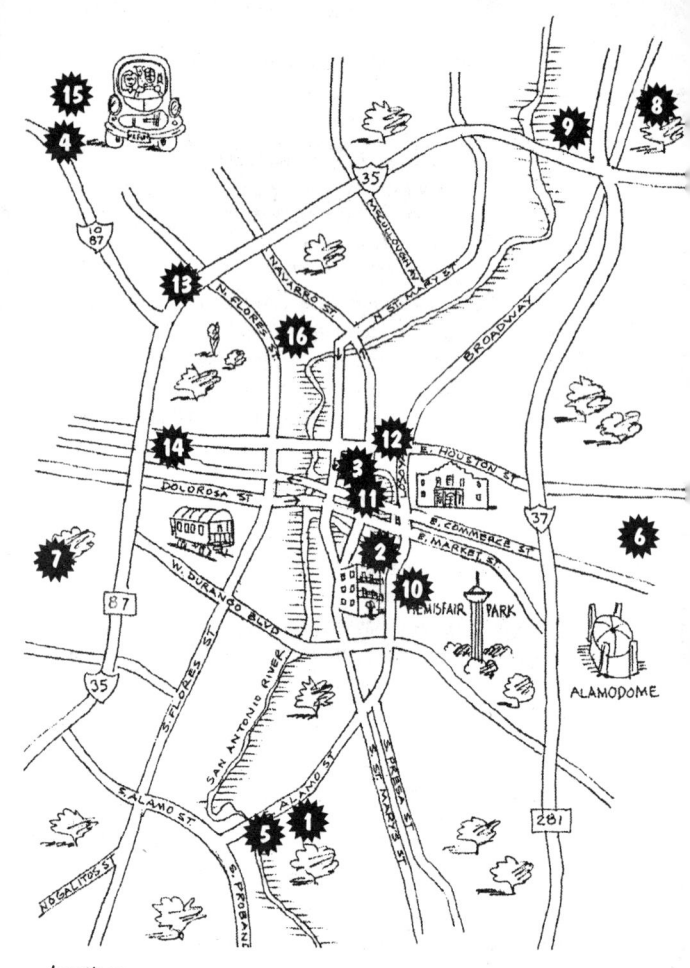

Locations

1. Alamo Street Restaurant and Theater
2. Arneson River Theatre
3. Arts! San Antonio
4. Ballet San Antonio
5. Blue Star Arts Complex
6. Carver Community Cultural Art Center
7. Guadalupe Cultural Arts Center
8. Harlequin Dinner Theater
9. Josephine Theater
10. Magik Children's Theater
11. Majestic Performing Arts Center
12. San Antonio Symphony
13. San Pedro Playhouse
14. "Spirit of Healing" by Jesse Treviño Mural at Santa Rosa's Children's Hospital
15. Steven Stoli Playhouse & The Backyard Theater
16. Southwest School of Arts and Crafts

Chapter 4
SAN ANTONIO'S GOT CULTURE AND TALENT
art, art galleries, operas, symphony and live theaters

Alamo Street Restaurant and Theater	82
Arneson River Theatre	83
Arts! San Antonio	84
Ballet San Antonio	85
Blue Star Arts Complex	86
Carver Community Cultural Art Center	87
Guadalupe Cultural Arts Center	88
Harlequin Dinner Theater	89
Josephine Theater	90
Magik Children's Theater	91
Majestic Performing Arts Center	92
San Antonio Symphony	93
San Pedro Playhouse	94
"Spirit of Healing" by Jesse Treviño Mural at Santa Rosa's Children's Hospital	95
Steven Stoli Playhouse & The Backyard Theater	96
Southwest School of Arts and Crafts	97

San Antonio's Got Culllture And Talent

ALAMO STREET RESTAURANT AND THEATRE

1150 S. Alamo Street, San Antonio 78204
210-271-7791

Dinner theater in an old historic church

Eat and be merry in this classy old church in the King William District. Listed on the National Register of Historic Places. The church sanctuary and Sunday school classrooms serve as the stage and dining hall. See comedies, dramas, and musicals to melodramas and murder mysteries. Cheer the heroes, boo at the villains, and question the suspicious for a delightful evening. Call for shows playing; many premier, at the Alamo Street Restaurant and Theatre, then travel elsewhere.

Reservations are a must—at least 2 weeks in advance for dinner and show. Celebrate a birthday, an anniversary, or some special occasion. Let them personalize the evening show for you. Tell them of your occasion when your make a reservation.

Use the theatre for social gatherings. Book a party and get a discount for groups over 20. Call for more details. The old church opens for lunch during the week and dinner when a show is playing. Served buffet style, dinners include roast beef, ham, pastas, salads, and the like.

Lunch - Mon. – Fri. . . . . 11:30 am – 2 pm
Dinner - Fri. and Sat. . . . . 6 pm – 8 pm
Show - Fri. and Sat. . . . . 8 pm

Adults *(Shows only)* $12
Children (3 – 10) *(Shows only)* $6
Adults *(Dinner and Shows)* $25
Children under 10 *(Dinner and Shows)* .. $12.25

Directions - 1 mile south of HemisFair Plaza, .6 mile south of the

San Antonio's Got **Cullture And Talent**

ARNESON RIVER THEATRE
La Villita—on the River Walk
210-207-8610

Amphitheater on the River Walk

Grab a blanket or cushion and join the fun at the Arneson River Theatre, down on the River Walk. From the Arneson Amphitheater, watch a show across the river. See nightly shows during the summer with live music, dance, and a south-of-the-border flair—a must-see for any tourist or local.

Summertime includes shows from the following production companies: the Fiesta Flamenca on Sunday, Monday, and Tuesday nights, Fandango Folkloric Troupe on Wednesday, and Fiesta Rio del Noche on Thursdays, Fridays, and Saturdays.

Purchase tickets in the La Villita Historic District, at the Arneson River Theatre entrance.

Watch for other productions in the winter; performed less often.

Hours
Summer

Nightly . . . . 8 pm

Cost

Tickets . . . . $6 - $10

Directions

Enter at La Villita, located between S. Alamo and S. Presa Streets.

San Antonio's Got Cullture And Talent

ARTS! SAN ANTONIO
222 E. Houston Street, Suite 630
San Antonio 78205
210-226-2891

A presenting company in San Antonio

See their annual production of "Shakespeare in the Park" in the lovely San Antonio Botanical Gardens, free. Enjoy great entertainment such as **The Nutcracker**, Bill Cosby, or **RiverDance**. Their full season includes ballet, classical and chamber music, contemporary dance, and more from around the world.

Claiming no home, Arts of San Antonio stages their productions at different locations—at the Majestic Theater, at other theaters around town, or in parks. Buy tickets for their performances at the ticket office on 222 E. Houston or at any Ticketmaster outlet. Call for a schedule.

Hours
(Ticket Office)
Mon. – Fri. . . . . 9 am – 5 pm

Cost
Tickets range from $10 - $65

Directions
Located downtown on E. Houston between N. St. Mary's and Navarro Streets.

San Antonio's Got Cullture And Talent

BALLET SAN ANTONIO

4335 Vance Jackson
San Antonio
210-340-0607

San Antonio's got ballet

Attend the ballet school's demonstration and see their students perform. Children begin classes here at early ages. Many eventually become professional dancers. Open to the public; see students at all levels dance with their ballet company.

The ballet company's performances throughout the year include ***The Nutcracker*** during the holidays. See it performed in the Cockrell Theatre downtown. Call for their demonstration and performance schedules. For tickets, call Ticketmaster.

Interested in a seeing their school facilities? Ask them for a tour.

Hours

Call for schedule

Cost

(Demonstrations)
Free
Ticket for performances vary

Directions

To get to the studio from downtown, take I-10 West then 410 going east. Exit Vance Johnson and go left. Will be 2 blocks outside the Loop on the left behind McDonalds.

San Antonio's Got Cullture And Talent

BLUE STAR ARTS COMPLEX

1420 S. Alamo Street, San Antonio 78204
210-227-6960
www.blue-star.net

San Antonio's contemporary art community

If you love contemporary art, visit the Blue Star Complex. Old historic warehouses across the river from the King William district now house San Antonio's contemporary art community. See works of local, regional, national, and even international artists. Galleries, such as Art Space, attract art lovers across Texas to their monthly opening.

These warehouses consist of more than art galleries: studios, a restaurant, a theater, and even apartments. The following places highlight the area.

BLUE STAR ART SPACE

116 Blue Star, Building C, 210-227-6960
An art gallery featuring contemporary art.

SAN ANGEL FOLK ART, INC.

110 Blue Star, Studio 100, Building B, 210-226-6688
See Mexican folk art.

Hours
Hours to galleries vary
Wed. – Sun. .... Noon – 6pm

Cost
Free

Directions

Five minutes south of downtown. Take S. Alamo south 1.5 miles. It's south of the San Antonio River.

San Antonio's Got Culture And Talent

CARVER COMMUNITY CULTURAL CENTER

226 N. Hackberry Street, San Antonio 78202
210-207-7211

San Antonio's successful multicultural community center

Big name artists like Ella Fitzgerald, Duke Ellington, Count Basie, Louie Armstrong, and "Dizzy" Gillespie walked through these doors. The Carver Community Cultural Art Center traces it historic roots back before desegregation. It started in 1905 as a cultural center for the black community in San Antonio and now stands as a national model of a multicultural center.

Today, the Carver Community Cultural Center sponsors an annual season of performing and visual arts. Every year, it features more than 50 performances, 24 art exhibitions, and numerous classes for young artists. Teaching everything from dance to ceramics, the center supports numerous arts and cultural activities in the community.

Tour the center. Learn more about its rich cultural heritage and what it offers the community. Tours last approximately 20 minutes.

Hours

Mon. – Fri. . . . . 8 am – 5 pm

Cost

Free

Directions

Take E. Houston, going east from downtown to N. Hackberry and turn left (south). Will be between

San Antonio's Got Culture And Talent

GUADALUPE CULTURAL ARTS CENTER

1300 Guadalupe Street, San Antonio 78207
210-351-7787

San Antonio's Hispanic cultural arts center

The Guadalupe Cultural Arts Center is recognized nationally as a huge success. Dedicated to the arts and culture of the Chicano, Latino, and Native American people, this center's activities involve all the arts: dance, literature, media, music, theater, and visual arts.

Tour the center. See the historic theater, the gallery, the dance studio, and the art gallery. The 1.5 hour tour offers insights in to the area's history and the center's 18 years of success.

Visit the art gallery and the gift shop. Return for a performance at the amphitheater or a concert. Popular, well-known annual events, such as the Tejano Conjunto Festival celebrate Tejano sounds. Attend their Inter-American Bookfair and Literary Festival, gathering Spanish literature from around the world. CinFestival highlights up-and-coming Hispanic films.

Hours (Center)

Mon. – Fri. .... 10 am – 6 pm

Cost (Tour)

Adults $6
Children (12 and under) .... Free
Seniors $4

Directions

Take I-10 to I-35N, exit UTSA Downtown Campus. Go left on Durango, then left on Frio. Go right on Guadalupe (the next light). Cross a bridge and down two lights to Brazos. It's on the corner of Guadalupe and Brazos.

San Antonio's Got Cullture And Talent

HARLEQUIN DINNER THEATER

Building 2652 Harney Road
Fort Sam Houston, 78208
210-221-5953

Army base dinner theater open to the public

Get your reservation now. Tickets go quickly at the Harlequin Dinner Theater. Call a week or two in advance for your reservation. Producing plays for 24 years, the theater is located at Fort Sam Houston, a military base accessible to the public.

Dinner includes bread, all-you-can-eat soup and salad, a choice of 4 entrees and 3 desserts, and a drink. Entrees include roast beef, chicken, and fish dishes.

Simply **Wait 'til Dark** for favorites like Agatha Christi's murder mysteries, **I Hate Hamlet** and **The Man Who Came to Dinner.** The theater produces eight plays a year and offers a season pass. It opens for seating at 6:15 pm; dinner is served at 7 pm. The show begins at 8 pm.

Hours

Wednesday, Thursday, Friday, and Saturday evenings

Cost (includes dinner)

Wed. and Thursday	$18.95
Fri. and Sat.	$19.95

Directions

Accessible to the public, Fort Sam Houston is 10 minutes from downtown San Antonio. Take I-35N and exit Walters Street. Go left on Walters Street. It will take you onto the base. Walters Street changes to Scott Street. Follow to Harney Road and go right. Will be one-half block down on the right.

San Antonio's Got Cullture And Talent

JOSEPHINE THEATER

339 W. Josephine Street
San Antonio 78215
210-734-4646

Local theater flaunts local talent

All musicals—see five a year at the Josephine Theater. Many are award winning. Enjoy favorites like **My Fair Lady, 42nd Street,** and **Crazy for You**. The theater, built in 1945, features an art deco architecture.

On occasions, performances include dramatic classics. Call for their program schedule. The theater is situated near restaurants.

Hours

Fri. and Sat.	8:15 pm
Sunday	2:30 pm

Cost

Adults	$16
Seniors	$14
Students	$11
Children under 12	$8

Directions

Located between Broadway and N. St. Mary's Streets. From downtown, take Broadway north past I-35 to Josephine and go left.

San Antonio's Got Culllture And Talent

MAGIK CHILDREN'S THEATER

420 S. Alamo Street
San Antonio 78205
210-227-2751

A top-notch children's theater

Like magic, even moms and dads get caught up in the fun. See what's playing at the Magik Theater. Better yet, get a season pass. Based on popular well-known children's literature, their plays will delight the whole family.

Let the kids read the book then see the play—like **The Tale of a Fourth Grade Nothing** or **The Grinch**. Other favorite performances include originals like the **The Phantom of the Alamo**—a must-see. Ask to be on the mailing list to keep up with their season's programming.

Acting classes for children and summer camps are available. Call for details.

Hours

Tues. – Fri.	9:30 am and 11:30 pm
Saturday	1 pm and 4 pm

Cost

Adults	$7
Children (3 - 17)	$5.50
Children under 3	$2
Seniors 65+	$6

Directions

Located in HemisFair Park at S. Alamo and Nueva.

San Antonio's Got **Culture And Talent**

MAJESTIC PERFORMING ARTS CENTER

230 E. Houston
San Antonio 78205
210-226-3333 Tickets
210-223-4343 Times & Prices

San Antonio's elegant theater

At the Majestic Performing Arts Center, see San Antonio's finest—productions and theater. Presenting arts include a Broadway series, concerts, ballets, children's theater, Tejano music awards, and big-name performers. Majestic aptly describes this atmospheric theater, one of only few left. Architect John Eberson's design adds elegance to any performance. Opened in 1929, the Majestic brought air-conditioning to San Antonio. Recently restored, the theater remains San Antonio's chief center for social affairs. See a performance to see this theater.

Tours of the Majestic Theater are offered. Call Las Casa (210-223-4343) for times and prices.

Hours
(Box Office)

Mon. – Sat. .... 10 am – 5 pm

Cost
Vary according to the performance

Directions

On E. Houston between St. Mary's and Navarro Streets.

San Antonio's Got Cullture And Talent

SAN ANTONIO SYMPHONY
222 East Houston St. #200
San Antonio 78205
210-554-1010
www.sasymphony.org

San Antonio's symphony relates to its community

The symphony got its start —June 12, 1939— with a gathering of music lovers at the Sunken Garden Theater. Now celebrating 60 years of community performances, the symphony continues to move forward with full seasons of educational, classical, pops, family, and outreach concerts, over a hundred concerts each year. Enjoy the diversity their community-minded programs offer, from Beethoven to Dance Festivals. Holiday favorites include **Handel's Messiah, The Nutcracker,** Humperdinck's **Hansel and Gretel, A Night in Old Vienna.**

The Instrument Petting Zoo, part of the family Interactive Classics, allows hands-on experiences for your child. Handle and attempt to play instruments with a musician's supervision. A Family Pass costs $140. Call for details.

Hours
Call for the season schedule

Cost
Prices vary for packages and performances

Directions
The San Antonio Symphony performs most of its concerts in the beautiful Majestic Performing Arts Center located at 230 E. Houston. Check performing schedules for locations.

San Antonio's Got Cullture And Talent

SAN PEDRO PLAYHOUSE

800 W. Ashby, San Antonio
210-733-7258

Local talent performs classics and originals

See musical favorites such as the **Little Shop of Horrors, The King and I,** and **Man of La Mancha** at San Antonio's oldest community theater. Located in the city's oldest park. The San Pedro Playhouse's original works, like the comedy, **Daddy's Dying, Who's Got the Will**, about a wealthy Texas rancher who dies and leaves his heirs a bottle of live potion complete with the formula, still delights audiences.

Open to community involvement, the theater offers interactive plays in schools, like **Snow White and the Seven Dwarfs.** Children get opportunities to develop an interest in theater.

Hours

Box office hours

Tues. – Sat. . . . . 10am – 5pm

Cost

Adults . . . . $17 - 20
Children (under 8) $10
Students (under 25) $11
Seniors . . . . $2 discount

Directions

Traveling north on I-35 on the north side of downtown, get in the left-hand lane and continue on I-35 as it splits from I-10. Take the first exit, San Pedro Avenue, and go left. Continue on San Pedro Avenue for 1.5 miles to Ashby and go left. The parking lot will be on the left.

San Antonio's Got Cullture And Talent

"SPIRIT OF HEALING"
by Jesse Treviño
MURAL AT SANTA ROSA CHILDREN'S HOSPITAL

Houston Street—across from Market Square

Fantastic mural on local children's hospital

Perhaps you'll meet the artist of this masterpiece as he lunches across the street. See this impressive mural entitled "Spirit of Healing" on the side of the Santa Rosa Children's Hospital. Created by a famous well-known artist, Jesse Treviño, the mural, 90 feet high and 40 feet wide is one of the largest in North America and contains over 150,000 pieces of hand-cut ceramic tile.

Overlooking Milam Park, the mural depicts a child holding a dove with a guardian angel and a cross in the background. To portray the innocence of youth, affection, and gentleness, the artist used his 10-year-old son as a model. The dove symbolizes peace, love, freedom, and spirituality. Make this part of your sightseeing in San Antonio.

The artist, Jesse Treviño often lunches at Mi Tierra Café at Market Square. With a little luck, you may see him there.

Hours
Drive by and stop anytime.

Cost
Free

Directions
On the side of the Santa Rosa Children's Hospital,

San Antonio's Got Cullture And Talent

STEVEN STOLI PLAYHOUSE AND THE BACKYARD THEATER

11838 Wurzbach, San Antonio
210-408-0116

A theater for children and a theater for grown-ups

Children's plays sell out quickly at the Backyard Theater. Reservations for an annual favorite, ***Frosty's New Hat Adventures***, start in September. The Backyard Theater's list of dandy productions include plays like ***Humpty-Dumpty's Pumpkin Patch, The Three Pigs, The City Mouse and The Country Mouse, Aladdin,*** and ***Turkey in the Store***—a Thanksgiving special. Bring your blanket and wear comfortable clothes, kids sit on the floor. Ask to be on their mailing list.

For the grown-ups, the Playhouse seats about 80 people and features terrific shows. Enjoy the Playhouse's great variety of shows. Watch plays like ***Odd Couple— a female version, Match Makers, Driving Miss Daisy, Watching for MacArthur, War of the Worlds*** and ***Social Security***. Year-round performances, with local talent.

Backyard Theater Hours & Costs

Tuesday	10 am
Saturday	10 am and Noon
Children	$4.25
Adults	$3.50

Playhouse Hours & Costs

Friday	8am
Saturday	8 am and 2:30 pm
Adults	$15
Seniors & Groups 20+	$12

Directions - In the Elms Shopping Ctr, center of the second floor. Take I-10N to Wurzbach exit and go right (north) to Lockhill-Selma. Will be on the corner.

San Antonio's Got Cullture And Talent

SOUTHWEST SCHOOL OF ARTS AND CRAFTS

300 Augusta Street, San Antonio 78205
210-224-1848

A unique combination of contemporary art at an historic site

Only a few professional-level art schools in our nation such as the Southwest School of Arts and Crafts teach as a non-degree-granting institute. Housed in the old Ursuline Academy for girls built in 1843, the school offers fun contemporary art classes for everyone, including children. It recently opened its Navarro campus which quadrupled its exhibition space.

The center gives an interesting tour of the historic buildings that lasts approximately 20 minutes. You will want to visit the art galleries: the Emily Edwards Gallery and the Ursuline Gallery, featuring works of visiting artists, students, instructors, and artists-in-residence.

Eat lunch at the Copper Kitchen Restaurant, serving lunch weekdays from 10:30 am to 2 pm. Be sure to browse in the gift shop with unique art and craft items for sale—another fun thing to do.

Special events such as lectures, concerts, and gallery openings invite public attendance. In April, you will enjoy viewing the arts and crafts from all over the United States during the Fiesta Art Fair. See ceramics, furniture, jewelry, paintings, photographs, and other art.

Hours - *(Closed major holidays)*
Mon. – Sat. . . . . 10am – 5pm

Cost - Free

Directions - At the corner of Navarro and Augusta

Locations

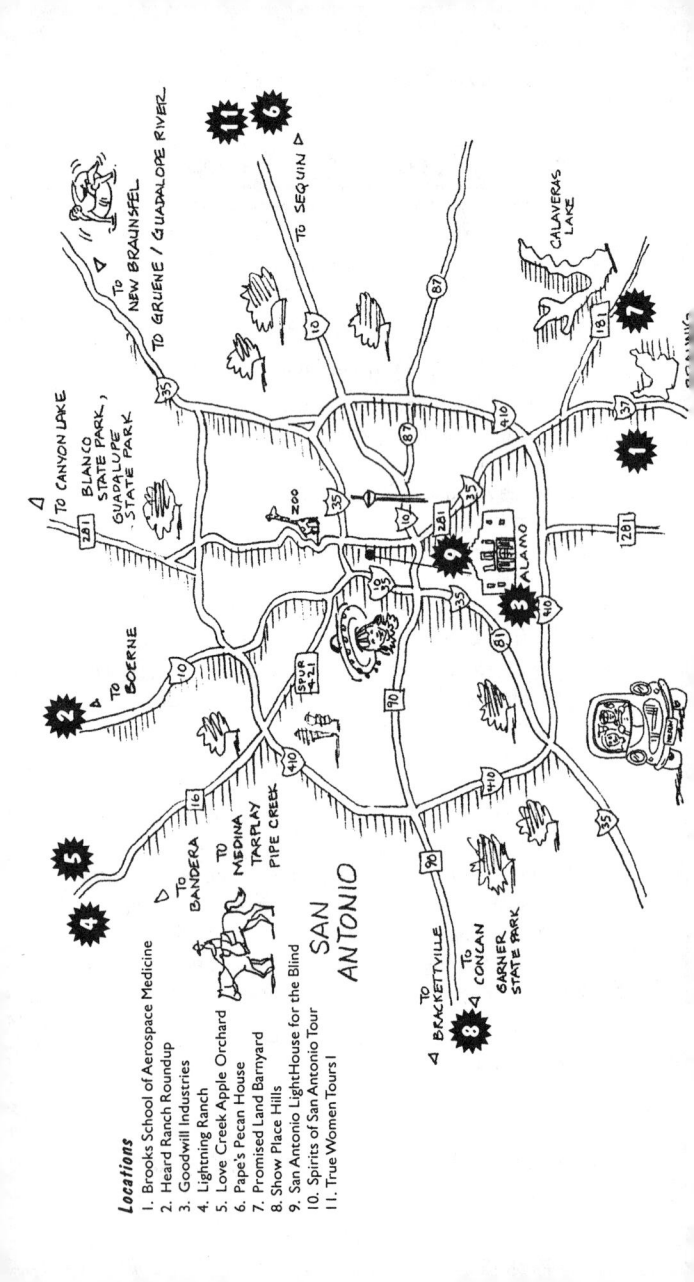

1. Brooks School of Aerospace Medicine
2. Heard Ranch Roundup
3. Goodwill Industries
4. Lightning Ranch
5. Love Creek Apple Orchard
6. Pape's Pecan House
7. Promised Land Barnyard
8. Show Place Hills
9. San Antonio LightHouse for the Blind
10. Spirits of San Antonio Tour
11. True Women Tours!

Chapter 5
TOURS AND MORE
special interests, field trips, group tours

Brooks School of Aerospace Medicine	100
Heard Ranch Roundup	101
Goodwill Industries	102
Lightning Ranch	103
Love Creek Apple Orchards	104
Pape's Pecan House	106
Promised Land Barnyard	107
Show Place Hills	108
San Antonio LightHouse for the Blind	109
Spirits of San Antonio Tour	110
True Women Tours	111

Tours And More

BROOKS SCHOOL OF AEROSPACE MEDICINE

Human Systems Center

Brooks Air Force Base
San Antonio 78235
210-536-3234

Only for group tours, call well in advance. Brooks School of Aerospace Medicine offers a popular tour for school groups, church groups, scouts, and out-of-towners, with groups of 10 or more. See where John Glenn trained for his flight in space. Tour includes the Human Systems Center's Armstrong Laboratory, the centrifuge, altitude chambers, and the flight school for nurses. Wear comfortable shoes.

Hours
Call for details

Cost
Free

Directions
On Brooks Air Force Base

Tours And More

HEARD RANCH ROUNDUP
P.O. Box 63, Fredericksburg 78624
210-824-3324 • 800-658-3773

Watch cowboys work cattle on a working ranch

In 1939, Cyrus Heard began ranching in the picturesque countryside of Fredericksburg, Texas, now one of our nation's fastest-growing tourist spots. Heard's grandson, a seventh generation Texas rancher, owns and operates the ranch. Using up-to-date technology, he raises high quality Herford cattle on the 10,000 acre ranch.

The Texas Hill Country ranch affords guests opportunities to see authentic cattle roundups, roping, and branding as real cowboys perform duties on a working ranch. Other enjoyable events include a country hayride, gun-fighting dramas, early morning campfire breakfasts, and visits to the historic 1893 Morris Ranch Schoolhouse, that serves as ranch headquarters. Afterwards, join the cowboys around a campfire for a chuckwagon barbecue supper: brisket, slaw, and beans with all the fixings. Activities at the ranch cater any age group.

Hours - Arrange for group tour

Cost - Varies according to group size

Directions

Take I-10 W towards Kerrville, exit US 87 to downtown Fredericksburg and turn left on Main Street. Take Main Street approximately 1.5 miles to N. Adams Street on Highway 16 and go left. Drive about 12 miles to the Morris Ranch Road; go right. Continue 2.4 miles until you see the Morris Ranch Schoolhouse on the right before the Pedernales River. Watch for signs for Heard Ranch.

Tours And More

GOODWILL INDUSTRIES

3830 Pleasanton Road
San Antonio 78221
210-924-8581

See what your donations of used items do for the community

Visit the largest Goodwill Industries in the state of Texas—doing over $5 million worth of business a year. They serve thousands of disabled people, placing many in regular employment. Take the 45-minute tour and get a first-hand look at how donations from the community change lives. Time spent here will be positive and upbeat; you'll leave with a new outlook on their purposes. Call and schedule a time to go.

Hours
(Tour can be arranged)

Mon. – Fri. . . . . 9 am – 3 pm

Cost
Free

Directions

From Interstate 35 South, take the Military Drive exit and go east to Pleasanton Road. Go south. Will be past McDonald's.

Tours And More

LIGHTNING RANCH
818 FM 1283
Pipe Creek 78063
830-510-4136

Enjoy a day of activities on a working ranch

See a family owned and operated working ranch in the heart of the Hill Country. Let their staff present your group, family or anyone with a day that includes horseback rides, hayrides, campfire roasts, trick roping, and western dancing. Learn to rope cattle, groom a horse, or be a blacksmith. The ranch offers guest overnight accommodations and overnight trail rides too. Call for more information.

Hours
Arrange for a group tour

Cost
Varies according to the group's size

Directions
Located 20 miles northwest of San Antonio. Take 1283 to Pipes Creek, go left .5 mile.

Tours *And More*

LOVE CREEK APPLE ORCHARDS, NATURE, AND BIRDING TOURS

112 Broadway
Medina 78055
210-589-2588 • 800-449-0882

Visit an apple orchard in the Hill Country

Check in at the Cider Mill and Country Store in downtown Medina before heading for the ranch tour. Delicious apple goodies of all kinds will get you in the spirit of this great adventure: fresh apples, sweet cider, apple pies, and apple products of all kinds.

Continue on to the apple orchards. Located in the heart of the scenic hill country, the 2000-acre ranch pioneered the Texas apple industry. You will see 14 different varieties of dwarf apple trees and the manufacturing of over 50 different apple items like jellies, jams, sauces, and butters. Love Creek Orchards is famous for their wonderful apples, apple pies, and apple ice cream. They feature apple tours year-round by reservations only with a minimum of 25 people. Tours also include apple cider and cookies. Ask about the sack lunch that they can provide for your group, making for a great picnic.

Remember to come back in October for the "Great Hill Country Pumpkin Patch." Your kids will enjoy picking a pumpkin for the holidays. Treat your family to this fun occasion.

Love Creek Orchards offers more than apple tours. Participate in one of the nature walks and birding tours that take you along Love Creek. Best time for the nature walk is in late October through mid-December. Enjoy learning about the fauna and flora indigenous to the Hill Country and the interesting geology of the area.

Tours And More

Take a birding tour in one of the best areas for finding interesting birds in South Texas. See birds like the golden-cheeked warbler, the black-capped vireo, the blue grosbeak, eastern bluebirds, painted and indigo buntings, to name a few. Call for more details.

Hours
Office Hours

Mon. – Fri. .... 8:30 am – 5 pm

Store

Mon. – Sat. .... 9 am – 5 pm
Sunday .... 10 am – 5 pm

Cost
(Discounts are available for school groups)
Apple orchards tours

Per person $4

Nature walking tours

Per person $25

Birding tours

Per person (minimum of 6 people) $15

Directions

Love Creek Orchards is located 60 miles northwest of San Antonio. Take I-10 West to Boerne. Exit Highway 46. Go left on Highway 46 and then right on Highway 16. Turn right at the light and continue 13 miles to Medina. Follow the signs for the Cider Mill. The ranch is 10 miles from Medina on Ranch Road 337. Will be on the right side of the road. Drive through the gate to the first house. The tour will begin here.

Tours And More

PAPE'S PECAN HOUSE
101 S. 123 Bypass
Seguin 78155
830-379-7442 • 888-688-7273

See pecan orchards and processing facilities

Family owned and operated, the famous Pape's Pecan House resides in the heart of the pecan orchard country. Pape's Pecan House processes an amazing 10,000 pounds of pecans every day. Open year-round, see how the Papes raise and process so many nuts. Take the walking tour of the orchards and facilities; you will find it enjoyable.

Pape's Pecan House makes pecans available for purchase. Buy them by the pound or by the truckload; they are the freshest available. Pape's Pecan House also retails other nuts, fruits, and candies. Plan to stock up. Ask for the recipe for Pape's Pralines.

This unique place prides itself on its fantastic collection of nutcrackers. They claim to have over 3000 different kinds from all over the world: hand-carved toy soldiers, Betel Cutters, and much more. Imagine seeing one over 6 feet tall.

Hours
Mon. – Fri. . . . . .8 am – 5 pm
Saturday .8 am – 3 pm

Cost
Free

Directions
Located 35 miles east of San Antonio. Take I-10 east approximately 30 miles to the 610-Mile Exit and go south to the 4th traffic light. Will be on the corner of 90A (Court Street) and 123 Bypass.

Tours **And More**

PROMISED LAND BARNYARD

Route 3 Box 197D
Floresville 78114
830-216-7182 ex. 105

Visit a working dairy farm

Feel like part of the family when you visit Promise Land Barnyard and spend an afternoon in the wholesome country atmosphere. Take the tour of a working dairy and creamery. See how they milk the Jersey cows, bottle the milk in old-fashioned glass bottles, make Supremely Creamy Ice Cream and other dairy products.

The farm offers hayrides through the rolling hills, a petting barn where kids get close and personal with the animals, and miniature golf on the 9-hole course. Be sure to browse through the gift shop, with country crafts and antique dairy items. Wear comfortable casual clothing and athletic shoes for this adventure.

Before going home, dine in the restaurant delicious home-cooked food. Have a great day in the country.

Hours

Daily .... 10 am – 5 pm

Cost

Tour / person $3
Hayride / per person $2

Directions

From downtown San Antonio, take I-37 south to Highway 181. Go south to Floresville and turn right (west) on Highway 97. Continue for 3.5 miles. Watch for the big red barn on the right.

Tours And More

SHOW PLACE HILLS
14693 Highway 90 West
San Antonio 78245
210-677-0000

Open-air tram tours of exotic animals

Make reservations for one of the most fun tours in San Antonio. A popular outing for school groups, scout groups, church groups, and tourists. See animals from six continents—zebras, camels, buffalo, deer, antelope, snakes, parrots, bugs, and more. Offers hands-on educational wildlife tours on a 250-acre ranch. Reservations are a must, make them in advance. Open only for groups of 15 or more during the week, weather permitting

Hours
Weekends by special appointment

Mon. – Fri. ....8 am – 5 pm

Cost

Adults $5
Children (2 – 17) $4
Children under 2 ....Free

Directions

Located on Highway 90, 7 miles west of Loop 410. The entrance will be on the right.

Tours And More

SAN ANTONIO LIGHTHOUSE FOR THE BLIND

2305 Roosevelt
San Antonio 78210
210-533-5195

Tour the industrial plant and rehabilitation center

Arrange to take a tour of a light industrial plant with modified equipment and a rehabilitation area for the blind. As an agency for the Texas Commission for the Blind, the LightHouse evaluates and trains as well as teaches literacy skills. Enjoy a better understanding of their operation and how people with visual problems can develop their abilities. Group tours last approximately 1.5 hours. Wear comfortable shoes, you will be walking. Call at least two weeks in advance.

Hours
(Arrange for a tour)
Mon. – Fri. .... 7:30 am – 4 pm

Cost
Free

Directions

From downtown, take St. Mary's south—it will turn into Roosevelt. Will be past the Riverside Golf Course.

Tours And More

SPIRITS OF SAN ANTONIO TOUR
210-493-2454

Enjoy an evening with
San Antonio's authority of spooks

Let Docia Williams, author of two historical guides to haunted places in Texas, take you to some of the spookiest places in San Antonio. Open for groups only of 20 or more. Smaller groups may join others if room is available. This is a popular activity, particularly around Halloween.

Tours are at night, last 3 hours, and include dinner at a haunted restaurant.

Hours
Call for meeting places, times, and reservations

Cost
Tour (includes dinner) .... $36 each

Tours And More

TRUE WOMEN TOURS

Seguin Convention and Visitors Bureau
427 N. Austin St.
Seguin 78155
800-580-7322

Tour the city made popular by the novel, *True Women*

Relive tales—the history and secrets of the frontier town of Seguin during the days of the Republic of Texas, as found in Janice Woods Windle's popular novel, **True Women.** Now a mini-series. Enjoy the tour with bridges much like those found in the movie **Bridges of Madison County.** Take a group tour provided with a step-on guide or the self-guided driving tour—exteriors only—with guide maps available at the visitor center. Plan to wear comfortable walking shoes and casual clothing. The tour lasts approximately 3 hours.

Hours
Group tour by appointment only

Cost
Guided tour

Guide	$50
Per person	$4

Directions

From downtown San Antonio, take I-10 East to Seguin—32 miles. Exit 609. Go right on Austin Street. The tourist information center will be on the left, before the Texas Theater, at the intersection of Austin and Ireland Streets.

Locations

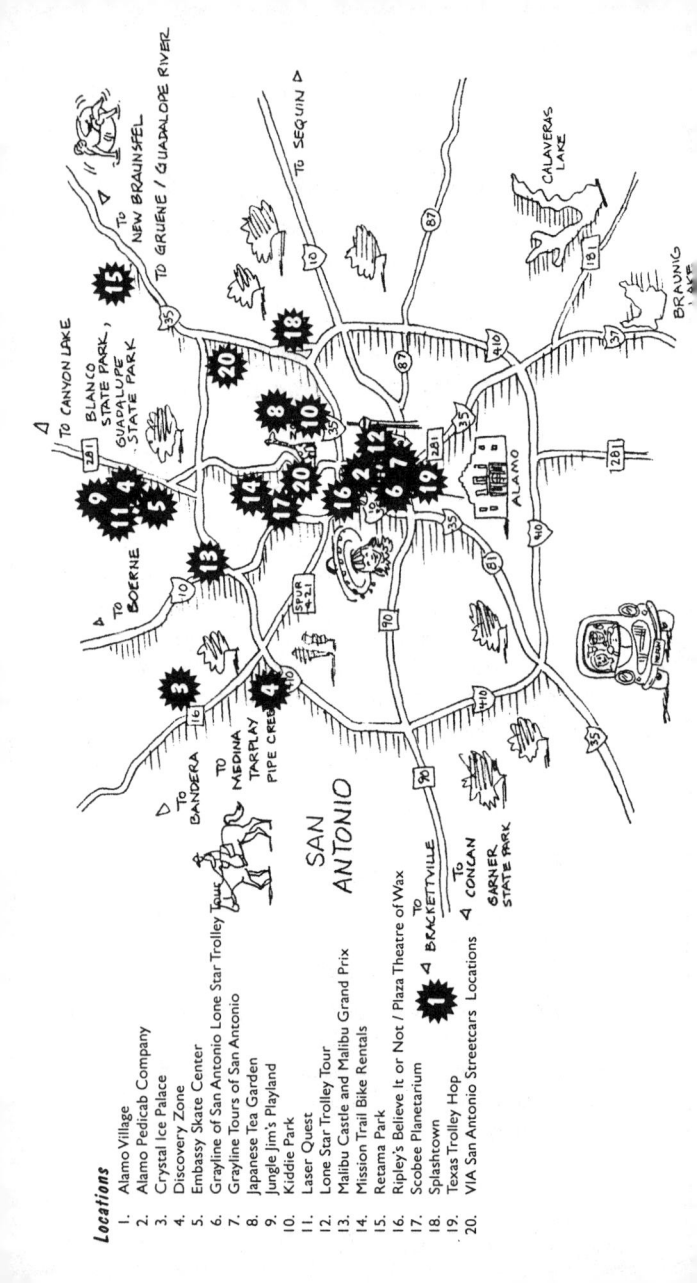

1. Alamo Village
2. Alamo Pedicab Company
3. Crystal Ice Palace
4. Discovery Zone
5. Embassy Skate Center
6. Grayline of San Antonio Lone Star Trolley Tour
7. Grayline Tours of San Antonio
8. Japanese Tea Garden
9. Jungle Jim's Playland
10. Kiddie Park
11. Laser Quest
12. Lone Star Trolley Tour
13. Malibu Castle and Malibu Grand Prix
14. Mission Trail Bike Rentals
15. Retama Park
16. Ripley's Believe It or Not / Plaza Theatre of Wax
17. Scobee Planetarium
18. Splashtown
19. Texas Trolley Hop
20. VIA San Antonio Streetcars Locations

Chapter 6
AMUSEMENT PARKS AND ATTRACTIONS
City Tours, Trolleys, and Streetcars

Alamo Village	114
Alamo Pedicab Company	115
Crystal Ice Palace	116
Discovery Zone	117
Embassy Skate Center	118
Grayline of San Antonio Lone Star Trolley Tour	119
Grayline Tours of San Antonio	120
Japanese Tea Garden	121
Jungle Jim's Playland	122
Kiddie Park	123
Laser Quest	124
Lone Star Trolley Tour	125
Malibu Castle and Malibu Grand Prix	126
Mission Trail Bike Rentals	127
Retama Park	128
Ripley's Believe It or Not / Plaza Theatre of Wax	129
Scobee Planetarium	130
Splashtown	131
Texas Trolley Hop	132
VIA San Antonio Streetcars	133

Amusement Parks, Attractions And More

ALAMO VILLAGE
P.O. Box 528, Brackettville 78832
830-563-2580

Movie making in West Texas

"Out in the middle of nowhere" takes on new meaning as you drive north of Brackettville on Highway 674. Keep going, seven more miles. You'll see where John Wayne recreated early frontier days in his movie **The Alamo**. To do so, he built an authentic replica of the Alamo. See this replica.

Used in moviemaking, the filming site includes a western frontier town with all that you'd expect to find: a jail, a hotel, a saloon, a bank, a general store, a livery stable, and more. Other movie favorites filmed here include **Lonesome Dove, Bandolero,** and **Streets of Laredo.**

Walk the streets, browse the gift shop, and visit the John Wayne Museum. See musicals and gunfights in the streets.

Go when the weather is cooler—October through April. Wear casual, comfortable clothes and shoes. Pack a cooler with food; eating establishments are few and far between.

Hours
Closed the week of Christmas

Daily .... 9 am – 6 pm

Cost

Adults $7
Children (11 - 6) $3.50
Children under 5 .... Free

Directions

From San Antonio take Highway 90 West 125 miles to Brackettville. Go 7 miles north on 674.

Amusement Parks,   *Attractions And More*

ALAMO PEDICAB COMPANY
151 W. Hermine Street
San Antonio 78212
210-710-3865

Get anywhere you want to go downtown with an Alamo Pedicab

Call an Alamo Pedicab and get around quickly. Go from any hotels to restaurants, to museums, or any other destination in no time without all the hassles of parking. Sit back and enjoy a pleasant ride while your friendly bike-pedaling chauffeur entertains you with historic tidbits.

Arrange to use pedicabs for other occasions: parties, weddings, romantic evenings, or any fun downtown excursion. Call and ask for more details.

Hours
Mon. – Fri. . . . . 5:30 am – 11 pm
Sat. and Sun. . . . . 11 am – 11 pm

Cost
Alamo Pedicabs work on tips

Directions
Call for a ride anywhere in the downtown area.

Amusement Parks, Attractions And More

CRYSTAL ICE PALACE
12332 W I-10 Site #12
San Antonio 78320
210-696-0006

San Antonio's only ice skating rink

Cheap skates for any cheap ice skater. Skate Monday or Tuesday nights from 7 pm – 9 pm for $2 at this well-run establishment with a friendly staff who like to assist patrons. Even small children can enjoy skating. The Crystal Ice Palace offers skates as small as a child's size eight and convenient skating hours day or evening.

Skates rent for $2 or bring your own.

Sign up for lessons, for your birthday party, or attend special events, like the Fiesta Competition that's held in April.

Hours

Mon. – Thurs.	11 am – 5:30 pm
	7 pm – 9 pm
Friday	11 am – 5 pm
	7:30 pm – Midnight
Saturday	1 pm – 5 pm
	7:30 pm – Midnight
Sunday	1 pm – 5 pm
	7 pm – 9 pm

Cost

Adults	$7
Children (4 – 12)	$5.90
Children (3 and under)	Free

Directions
Located at I-10 and De Zavala Road.

Amusement Parks,   *Attractions And More*

DISCOVERY ZONE

5751 NW Loop 410, San Antonio 78238
210-681-3300
13722 Embassy Row, San Antonio 78216
210-494-1226

Fun activities for young children

Little things make the difference at this well-thought-out establishment, with entertaining activities any child will love. Even toddlers have their own play area. What's fun? Tickets accumulated in any amount redeem for prizes.

Stay as long as you like. You'll find the food reasonably priced. Parents supervise their child's play. Wear comfortable casual clothes and athletic shoes.

Hours

Mon. – Thurs. . . . . 10 am – 8 pm
Fri. – Sat. . . . . 10 am – 9 pm
Sunday . . . . 11 pm – 7 pm

Cost

Children under 38 inches $4.99
Children over 38 inches $6.99

Directions

#1 The center at NW Loop 410 and Bandera is located outside the loop. Exit Leon Valley.

#2 The center on Embassy Row is located at Highway 281 and Bitters Road. Exit Bitters Road and go left. Go left on Embassy road. Will be on your left.

Amusement Parks, Attractions And More

EMBASSY SKATE CENTER

606 Embassy Oaks
San Antonio
210-495-2525

San Antonio's new roller skating rink

Skate with a view. The Embassy Skate Center's large windows make it a unique place to go skating.

Family oriented, the rink offers an afternoon of fun at a reasonable admission that includes the skates if you don't plan to bring your own. Children ages four and older will enjoy the activities. With refreshments and video games the center provides a great place for birthday parties. Or sign up for skating classes and private lessons. Call for more details.

Hours

(Extended hours in the summer)

Daily .... 3 pm – 6 pm
Sat. and Sun. .... 1 pm – 5 pm
Fri. and Sat. .... 7:30 pm – 11 pm

Cost

(Includes skates)

Weekdays $3.50
Weekends $5.00

Directions

From downtown, take Highway 281 N. and exit Bitters Road. Go left on Bitters to the first stop light then left on Embassy Row. Located behind the Embassy 14 Movie Theater.

Amusement Parks, Attractions And More

GRAYLINE OF SAN ANTONIO LONE STAR TROLLEY TOURS

217 Alamo Plaza, San Antonio
210-226-1706

See San Antonio on a trolley

Hop on the trolley all you want, all day long. Board a replica, turn-of-the-century trolley for a personal guided tour of historic San Antonio. When the tour is over, you'll have an idea of what the city offers. Trolleys leave every 30 minutes with stops along the way. Tickets include "off and on" privileges good for the day. Simply catch the next trolley and continue on with the tour. Go early; plan to spend most of the day. You'll find this to be an excellent way to see downtown.

The trolley will stop at the following: the Alamo, the Hertzberg Circus Museum, Arneson River Theatre, La Villita, Yanaguana River Cruise, Institute of Texan Cultures, Tower of the Americas at HemisFair Park, Mission San Jose, Mission Concepcion, Lone Star Buckhorn Museum, King William Historic District, San Fernando Cathedral, Spanish Governor's Palace, and Market Square. Have fun sightseeing San Antonio.

Hours & Costs

Summer hours extend until 6 pm

Daily	10 am – 5 pm
Adults	$9.50
Children (3 – 12)	$4.50
Children under 3	Free

Directions

Across from the Alamo, at Ripley's Believe It or Not.

Amusement Parks, Attractions And More

GRAYLINE TOURS OF SAN ANTONIO

217 Alamo Plaza, Suite B, San Antonio 78205
210-226-1706 • 800-472-9546

Enjoy one of these tours

Want to see more than just San Antonio? San Antonio Gray Line Tours offers a wide variety of tours to choose from—each having a particular focus. Tours include Austin, the Texas Hill Country, and Mexico.

Here's a brief sampling of what they offer. Ask about the one that interests you.

The Mission Trail
The Alamo and the Spanish Colonial Missions

San Antonio Sampler
Highlights, Homes, and History

Alamo City Grand Tour
A combination tour plus the Yanaguana River Cruise

Texas Hill Country Escape
LBJ Homesites and Texas Countryside

Tales of Two Cities
Laredo, Texas and Nuevo Laredo, Mexico

Experience Austin
The Texas Capitol

Tours depart from and return to the Alamo Plaza. Or arrange to be picked up and dropped off at your hotel. The cost and length of each tour varies. Some tours leave as early as 8:30 am and the latest returns at 6:30 pm. Prices range between $22 and $38 for an adult and $11 to $19 for children under 12. Lunch is not included in the tour.

JAPANESE TEA GARDEN

3800 N. St. Mary's Street
San Antonio 78212
210-207-8480

Enjoy the garden's serenity

Creating something this unique out of an old rock quarry was a novel idea. See a Japanese garden, with winding pebbled walkways, stone bridges, tranquil pools, and even a 60-foot waterfall. Once supplying limestone for the State Capitol Building in Austin, the old quarry was built in 1917 with prison labor. Now open after extensive renovations, the garden makes a delightful place to visit.

After the Japanese attack on Pearl Harbor, the garden's name changed to the Chinese Sunken Garden. The city finally restored its original name in 1983. Notice the Chinese-looking entrance; it now reminds us of those days.

Take the kids. They will enjoy the stroll. Wear comfortable athletic shoes. You'll climb lots of steps and pathways but will find it inaccessible to strollers.

Hours

Daily .... 8 am - dusk

Cost

Free

Directions

At the northwestern edge of Brackenridge Park.

Amusement Parks, Attractions And More

JUNGLE JIM'S PLAYLAND
13311 San Pedro
San Antonio 78216
210-490-9595

Delight your kids at this fun indoor theme park

At Jungle Jim's Playland, parents join in the fun for free. Entertain your kids for hours at this indoor amusement park. It offers rides, skill games, slides, ball pits, and even big-ticket payoffs for prizes of your choice.

Some activities require socks, others shoes. Plan to stay as long as you'd like, tickets are good for the entire day. Ask about having your birthday party at Jungle Jim's; it is a great place to entertain your friends.

Hours
(Summer Hours 10 am – 9 pm)
Mon. – Thurs. . . . . 11 am – 9 pm
Fri. and Sat. . . . . 10 am – 10 pm
Sunday . . . . 11 am – 8 pm

Cost
Adults . . . . Free
Unlimited rides and soft play
Children (2 – 12) Weekdays $5.99
Children (2 – 12) Weekends $6.99

Directions
Located on the Highway 281 at Bitters Road, north of downtown San Antonio.

Amusement Parks, *Attractions And More*

KIDDIE PARK
3015 Broadway
San Antonio 78209
210-824-4351

Small outdoor amusement park for younger children

Visit the oldest amusement park in the United States. Open year round, weather permitting, Kiddie Park's rides will be a hit with any kids ages 2 to 12. Enjoy traditional amusement park rides, like a roller coaster, a Ferris wheel, a merry-go-round, boat rides, airplane rides, cars, and more. Built in 1918, the original merry-go-round continues to operate. There are arcade games, too.

Concession stands add to the fun or bring along a cooler of food for a picnic. Parking is free. Park either on Avenue B or on Broadway.

Hours
Daily .... 10 am – dark

Cost
1 ticket .... $.70
5 tickets $3.25
Unlimited rides/person $5.99

Directions
Located on the corner of Broadway and Mulberry. From downtown, simply take Broadway north towards Brackenridge Park.

Amusement Parks, Attractions And More

LASER QUEST
606 Embassy Oaks
San Antonio 78216
210-499-4400

Play a modern game of tag

Imagine yourself wandering through this awesome maze, your heart pounding as you seek out your opponent in this incredible hi-tech game of tag. You're surrounded with action as the fun intensifies. You aim; you fire; you're fired upon.

Your family will find this an unforgettable adventure. Anyone can play the game—if you're big enough to wear the laser pack (children ages 6 or older). Games last approximately 20 minutes.

Play laser tag for your birthday party, with corporate groups, clubs, churches, and scout troops. It offers team-building experiences. Ask about customizing the game. Remember to wear comfortable clothes and athletic shoes. You'll see what computers have done to a simple game of tag. Ask about memberships that include discounts at other local attractions and eateries in the area, special game times and rates.

Hours
Sun. – Thur. . . . . 3 pm – 10 pm
Fri. – Sat. . . . . 3 pm – Midnight

Cost
Per game $6.50

Directions

Behind the Embassy 14 Movie Theater on Highway 281 and Bitters Road. From downtown, take Highway 281 N. and exit Bitters Road. Go left on Bitters to the first stop light then left on Embassy Row.

Amusement Parks, *Attractions And More*

LONE STAR TROLLEY TOUR
217 Alamo Plaza, San Antonio
210-226-1706
(Boarding and tickets from Ripley's Believe It or Not)

San Antonio in a nutshell

Board a replica, turn-of-the-century trolley for a personal guided tour of historic San Antonio. Tours begin downtown, across from the Alamo at the Ripley's Believe It or Not and the Plaza Theater of Wax. Trolleys leave every 30 minutes. Tickets include "off and on" privileges good for the day. Simply catch the next trolley and continue on with the tour. Go early; plan to spend most of the day. You'll find this to be an excellent way to see downtown.

You'll enjoy visiting the following: the Alamo, the Hertzberg Circus Museum, Arneson River Theatre, La Villita, Yanaguana River Cruise, Institute of Texan Cultures, Tower of the the Americas at HemisFair Park, Mission San Jose, Mission Concepcion, Lone Star Buckhorn Museum, King William Historic District, San Fernando Cathedral, Spanish Governor's Palace, and Market Square. Have fun sightseeing San Antonio.

Hours & Costs
Summer hours extend until 6 pm

Daily .... 10 am – 5 pm

Adults $9.50
Children (3 – 12) $4.00
Children under 3 .... Free

Directions
Across from the Alamo.

Amusement Parks, *Attractions And More*

MALIBU CASTLE AND MALIBU GRAND PRIX

3330 Cherryridge, San Antonio 78320
210-341-6664 Miniature golf
210-341-2500 Grand Prix racing

Two outdoor attractions offer miniature golf and stock car racing

Play miniature golf on the two 9-hole courses featuring a fantasy atmosphere. Combine this with bumper boats, video games, batting cages, and sprint cars for a great afternoon or evening of fun.

Next door, race three sizes of racecars along the mile track. The Virage is a ¾ scale formula racecar. The Grand Virage, the larger car, seats two. The third car, the Mini Virage allows kids 8 years of age or 54 inches or taller to experience the fun.

Hours

Closed Mondays & Tuesdays in the winter

Mon. – Thurs.	4 pm - 9 pm
Friday	Noon - Midnight
Saturday	11 am – Midnight
Sunday	Noon – 10 pm

Cost - Miniature golf

Adults	$5.95
Children under 13	$4.95
Children under	Free

Grand Prix Racing
Prices vary according to car

Directions

From downtown take I-10 West to the Callaghen exit and go right on Callaghen, turn right on Pine Brook, then a right on Briaridge Drive. Turn left on Cherry Ridge.

Amusement Parks, Attractions And More

MISSION TRAILS BIKE RENTALS

151 W. Hermine
San Antonio 78212
210-805-8937

See the historic missions on bikes

Burn off those enchiladas, refried beans, and the tacos while sightseeing San Antonio. See the Alamo City in a new way—on a bike. Mission Trail Bike Rentals allows you to bike to the sites with an easy-to-follow map that includes popular restaurants, antique shops, attractions and museums within a comfortable pedaling distance.

Arrange for the bikes to be delivered to your hotel or wherever you prefer. Ask about customizing a bike ride or taking a guided tour of the Spanish Missions. Used by missionaries and Indians over 250 years ago, the mission trail makes for a fun and educational day of biking.

Bike at your own pace. Recommended for teenagers and adults; it may be too strenuous for younger children. Bike rentals include the bike, the lock, a helmet, a bottle of water, a map of downtown and the missions. Bikes are delivered and picked up at no extra charge. Have fun.

Hours

Operates 7 days a week

Cost

Bike/day $19

Amusement Parks, Attractions And More

RETAMA PARK
One Retama Parkway, Selma 78154
210-651-7000

Visit one of San Antonio's newest attractions

Monitors make horse racing more entertaining. With a world-class track, the park features year-round horse racing, live or simulcast from other tracks throughout the country. Enjoy the races from the second floor grandstand, from the fourth floor air-conditioned clubhouse, or from ground level. Televised races provide opportunities to wager on horses anywhere in the United States. Retama Park offers easy viewing from hundreds of monitors throughout the facility.

The wagering program comes with simple instructions, making it easy for beginners. Also available in Spanish. Call and ask about group rates for 20 people or more.

Suit the occasion with dining at a fine restaurant overlooking the tracks or eating the usual chili cheese dogs and tacos at the fast food court.

Hours - Times vary, call for the schedule

Cost

General Admission (live racing)	$2.50
Clubhouse Admission	$3.50
Simulcast Admission	$1
Children under 15 (with adult)	Free
Seniors over 62:	
General Admission	$1.50
Clubhouse Admission	$2.50
Parking	$1

Directions

Located 15 minutes north of downtown San Antonio. Take I-35 and exit 174-A, north of Loop 1604.

Amusement Parks, *Attractions And More*

RIPLEY'S BELIEVE IT OR NOT PLAZA THEATRE OF WAX

301 Alamo Plaza, San Antonio
210-224-9299

See the unbelievable

You'll find two attractions at the same location. See them both and get a discount. Based on the original television series and the travels of the famous cartoonist, Ripley's Believe It or Not exhibits the strange and exotic from around the world. With 8 different galleries and over 500 exhibits, the attraction includes a man with double pupils in each eye, a hand-written Bible, a beautiful 5-foot papier-mâché Madonna, and the world's tallest man. Experience the hurricane simulator, with winds over a 55 mph.

The Plaza Theatre of Wax features over 250 life-size figures. Look for Kevin Costner, Denzel Washington, Jim Carrey, Whoopie Goldberg, Brad Pitt, Julia Roberts, and Captain Picard. Bring the camera; you'll enjoy posing with the stars. The theatre divides into themes of Hollywood, Horror, History, and Religion.

Hours

Winter *(Closed Christmas Day)*
Sun. – Thurs. . . . . 9 am – 7 pm
Fri. – Sat. . . . . 9 am – 10 pm

Summer
Daily . . . . 9 am – 10 pm

Cost

Adults $11.95
Children (4 – 12) $7.95
Seniors $10.95

Directions - Across from the Alamo

Amusement Parks, Attractions And More

SCOBEE PLANETARIUM at San Antonio College

1300 San Pedro Avenue
San Antonio
210-733-2910

See a planetarium show, then visit the observatory

Enjoy trekking through the solar system or gazing at the night's sky constellations every Friday night. Attendees of the evening's last performance get an additional treat. Weather permitting, they can stay for more at the observatory.

Shows last approximately one hour and allow children as young as 6 years of age. Wear comfortable casual clothing.

Offering shows for kids, the planetarium includes children ages 4 and older. Shows make popular field trips for school groups. Call for more details. Please note that the planetarium closes mid-July through August each year.

Hours

Fridays . . . . 6 pm – 9 pm

Cost

Free

Directions

North of downtown. From I-35N exit San Pedro Avenue and go north (left). Will be past E. Park Street.

Amusement Parks, Attractions And More

SPLASHTOWN
3600 I-35 North
San Antonio 78219
210-227-1400

Have a fun day at this water park

Want to save a bundle? Remember to bring an empty can or some other proof of purchase from any Country Time Lemonade product and receive half-off admission before 5 pm. One can will include half-off admission for up to six adults and children.

Besides offering a great bargain, the water park offers something fun for everyone: body slides, tube rides, a wave pool, and the popular Kids' Kove. You'll find the Lone Star Luge, a huge slide with twists and turns, a hit with the family.

Bring a cooler of food for the picnic area adjacent the park. Life jackets and tubes come with the admission price. The park offers rental lockers and a concession stand. Watch for special events and concerts. Parking is free.

Hours
Sun. – Thurs. . . . . 11 am – 9 pm
Fri. and Sat. . . . . 11 am – 10 pm

Cost
Adults $17.99
Children under 4 feet $12.95
Children under age 2 . . . . Free
Seniors 65+ . . . . Free

Directions
North of downtown San Antonio on I-35 North. Take the Splashtown Road exit #160. Will be on the right.

Amusement Parks, Attractions And More

TEXAS TROLLEY HOP
216 Alamo Plaza, San Antonio
210-225-8587 Information
210-212-5395 Group Reservations

A fun and convenient way to see San Antonio

The Texas Trolley offers two 60-minute tours aboard their air-conditioned and heated trolleys. Choose either the Historic Tour or the Uptown Tour. If that's a difficult decision, they offer both at a discount. Better yet, for a few dollars more, the Hop Pass gives you unlimited reboarding privileges at any of the Texas Trolley Hop Stops. Spend the day sightseeing at the places that interest you.

The Historic Tour includes the Alamo, the IMAX Theatre, the River Walk, HemisFair Park, Mission San Jose and Mission Concepcion, the Lone Star Buckhorn Museums, Market Square, San Fernando Cathedral, and La Villita.

On the Uptown Tour, you will see Ft. Sam Houston, the San Antonio Botanical Gardens, the McNay Art Museum, Olmos Park, the San Antonio Zoo, Brackenridge Park, the Witte Museum, and the San Antonio Museum of Art.

Daily Hours . . . . 9:30 am

60-Minute Historic Tour or 60-Minute Uptown Tour Costs
Adults $9.95
Children 3-11 . . . . $4.95
Adults (with Hop Pass) $11.95
Children (with Hop Pass) $5.95

One-day Combination Costs—includes Hop Pass
Adults $16.95
Children 3-11 . . . . $8.95

Two-day Combination Costs—includes Hop Pass for two days
Adults $19.95
Children 3-11 . . . . $9.95

Directions - Board trolley at the Alamo Visitor Center at the Menger Hotel next to the Alamo.

Amusement Parks, Attractions And More

VIA SAN ANTONIO STREETCARS
(VIA Metropolitan Transit)

112 N. Soledad (downtown office), San Antonio
210-362-2000
210-362-2020 Customer information

800 W. Myrtle, San Antonio
210-227-5371

Crossroads Park-and-Ride
In the Crossroads Mall Parking Lot
210-735-3317

Check out San Antonio's streetcar system

Cheap and easy. Anyone looking for a convenient way to get around San Antonio will enjoy the streetcar system. Not only is it the best way to get around downtown, fares cost only $.50. Routes circulate popular tourist destinations, shopping centers, and city parks. Enjoy riding the open-air, rubber-tired replicas of the turn-of-the-century trolleys that operated in San Antonio 50 years ago.

Streetcars operate from early morning until late in the evening. Wait at a stop no longer than about 10 minutes. Pay with cash, streetcar tokens, or ride all you want for the day for $4 with a Streetcar Pass.

Schedules and route information can easily be obtained at one of their offices or at the Alamo Visitor Center across from the Alamo.

VIA Transit System offers schoolchildren opportunities for field trips by way of their bus system called VIA's Class Pass. Call for more information, 210-362-2370. The program provides a trip planning guide and a list of popular field trips in the city area.

Locations

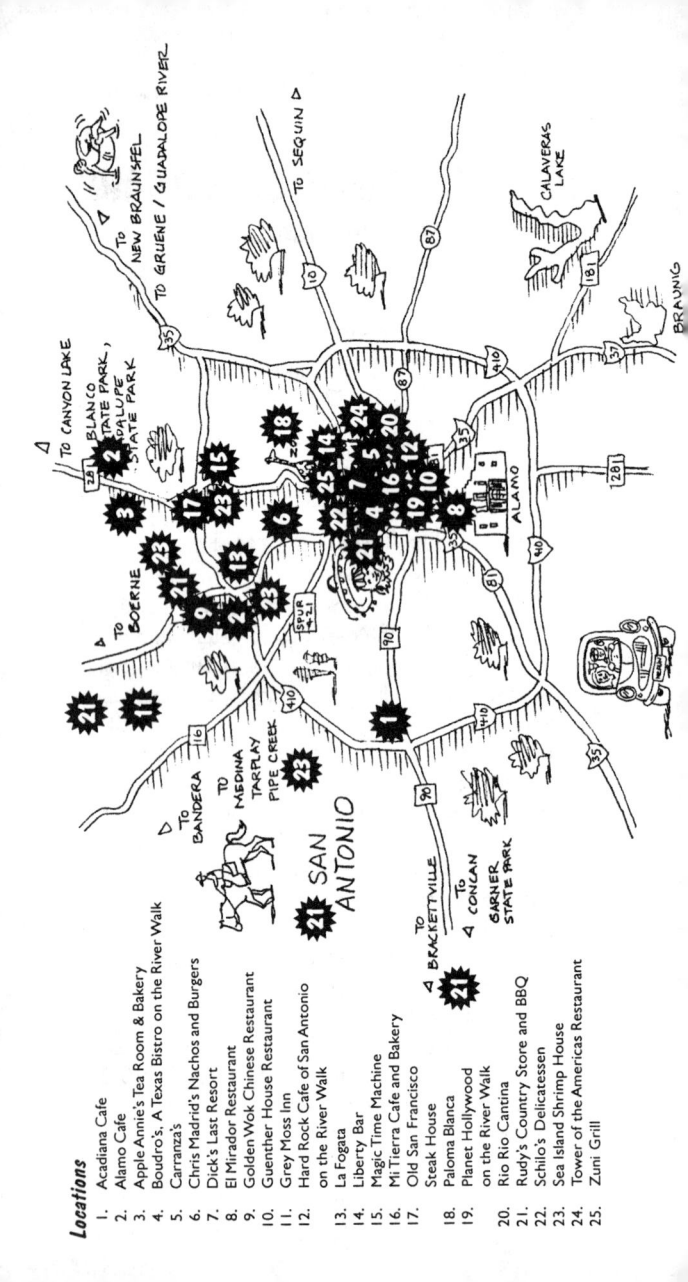

1. Acadiana Cafe
2. Alamo Cafe
3. Apple Annie's Tea Room & Bakery
4. Boudro's, A Texas Bistro on the River Walk
5. Carranza's
6. Chris Madrid's Nachos and Burgers
7. Dick's Last Resort
8. El Mirador Restaurant
9. Golden Wok Chinese Restaurant
10. Guenther House Restaurant
11. Grey Moss Inn
12. Hard Rock Cafe of San Antonio on the River Walk
13. La Fogata
14. Liberty Bar
15. Magic Time Machine
16. Mi Tierra Cafe and Bakery
17. Old San Francisco Steak House
18. Paloma Blanca
19. Planet Hollywood on the River Walk
20. Rio Rio Cantina
21. Rudy's Country Store and BBQ
22. Schilo's Delicatessen
23. Sea Island Shrimp House
24. Tower of the Americas Restaurant
25. Zuni Grill

Chapter 7
WHERE TO EAT?

Acadiana Cafe	136
Alamo Cafe	137
Apple Annie's Tea Room & Bakery	138
Boudro's, A Texas Bistro on the River Walk	139
Carranza's	140
Chris Madrid's Nachos and Burgers	141
Dick's Last Resort	142
El Mirador Restaurant	143
Golden Wok Chinese Restaurant	144
Guenther House Restaurant	145
Grey Moss Inn	146
Hard Rock Cafe of San Antonio on the River Walk	147
La Fogata	148
Liberty Bar	149
Magic Time Machine	150
Mi Tierra Cafe and Bakery	151
Old San Francisco Steak House	152
Paloma Blanca	153
Planet Hollywood on the River Walk	154
Rio Rio Cantina	155
Rudy's Country Store and BBQ	156
Schilo's Delicatessen	157
Sea Island Shrimp House	158
Tower of the Americas Restaurant	159
Zuni Grill	160

Where To Eat?

ACADIANA CAFE
1289 Southwest Loop 410
San Antonio
210-674-0019

Cajun

This popular Cajun restaurant proves that not all the spicy food in San Antonio is Tex-Mex. Parents needn't worry though. There's plenty here to keep all ages happy.

Mouth-watering, buttery biscuits served with honey will have kids and adults begging for more. Fried catfish and crispy hush puppies are top-notch.

During the holidays, call ahead and see if it's one of the days that Acadiana is serving its famous deep-fried turkey. Whole turkeys also are available year-round. (advance ordering required).

Hours
Sun.-Thur. .... 11 am-10 pm
Fri. and Sat. .... 11 am-11 pm

Cost
$6 -15

Directions
From downtown, take 410 West, exit #8 (Lakeside Parkway). Continue on the access road. Will be at the West Lakes Theater's parking lot.

Where To Eat?

ALAMO CAFE

10060 I-10 West, San Antonio
210-691-8827
and
14250 Highway 281 North, San Antonio
210-495-2233

Mexican

Even if these restaurants weren't so well placed (one in the airport vicinity, the other near Six Flags Fiesta Texas), they'd be worth the drive. Alamo Café knows how to keep the chips, salsa, and warm tortillas coming and the beverages (including soft drinks) constantly refilled.

Best bets include an incomparable tortilla soup and chicken fajita combo. Kids go for their mild but tasty version of chile con queso. Chicken fried steak is oversized and the perfect contrast between crispy breading and tender interior. Save room for their famous margarita pie. No reservations.

Hours

Mon. - Thurs. .... 10:45 am - 11 pm
Fri. - Sat. ....10:45 am - Midnight

Cost - $6 -15

Directions

For the restaurant at 10060 I-10, take I-10 West to the Huebner exit (outside Loop 410) and take the turnaround to cross back over I-10. The restaurant will be approximately .5 mile on the right on the access road.

For the restaurant at 14250 Highway 281 North, take Highway 281 North to the Winding Way/Oak Shadows exit (outside Loop 410). The restaurant will be approximately .25 mile on the right side of the access road.

Where To Eat?

APPLE ANNIE'S TEA ROOM & BAKERY

555 Bitters Road
San Antonio
210-491-0226

American

Located in the midst of Artisan's Alley, a delightful mix of some 20 quaint shops (kids will love The Stamping Factory). This tearoom has as its motto, "You can't leave hungry."

A savory cheese appetizer greets guests as they're seated. From there, pick between homemade soups, savory salads and sandwiches, and daily specials such as King Ranch chicken. Sinfully rich desserts, including the tearoom's signature Sawdust Pie and Apple Crunch Cake, are the perfect ending. Open daily for lunch until 2:30 pm (3 pm on the weekend) and for desserts until 5:30 pm.

Hours

Mon. – Fri. . . . . 11 am – 2:30 pm
Sat. – Sun. . . . . 11 am – 3 pm

Cost
$5-8

Directions

Take 281 North to Bitters Road and go left one mile. Will be on the right.

Where To Eat?

BOUDRO'S, A TEXAS BISTRO ON THE RIVER WALK

421 E. Commerce
San Antonio
210-224-8484

American

Considered the star in the crown that is San Antonio's river dining, Boudro's is the perfect place to leisurely watch River Walk crowds while you dine in casual comfort.

Order guacamole and get ready for the kids to be fascinated as it's prepared tableside. Who knows? With that kind of incentive, they may even take to the kitchen when they get home.

Hours

Sun. - Thurs. .... 11 am - 11 pm
Fri. - Sat. .... 11 am - Midnight

Cost

$12 - 20

Directions

Located in the middle of the River Walk, between the Hyatt Regency and the Hilton Palacio Del Rio.

Where To Eat?

CARRANZA'S

701 Austin St.
San Antonio
210-223-0903

Barbecue/Italian/Mexican/Seafood

Family can't settle on whether to eat seafood, Italian, Mexican, or barbecue? Carranza's lets you have all of the above, and then some.

Located in a charmingly restored stone building near downtown, Carranza's began serving barbecue out of a tiny grocery store and grew from there. Seafood entrees—particularly sea cakes served with dual sauces—are incomparable. Kids will love their spaghetti and meatballs. An outpost at 2908 N. St. Mary's St. (210-735-6801) serves barbecue only.

Hours

(Closed Sunday)
Lunch
Mon. – Fri. .... 11 am – 2 pm
Dinner
Mon. – Thur. .... 5 pm – 10 pm
Fri, and Sat. .... 5 pm – 11 pm

Cost

$6 – 28.50

Directions

From downtown, take Broadway north to Jones and go right. Cross Alamo and go left on Austin. Will be on the left, look for the 1st old limestone building (Carranza's Grocery and Market).

Where To Eat?

CHRIS MADRID'S NACHOS AND BURGERS

1900 Blanco Road
San Antonio
210-735-3552

Burgers/Mexican

Burgers and nachos—need we say more? Only that these are some of the juiciest, floppiest, tastiest burgers you'll ever see, including the beanburger loaded with refried beans, cheese, and crunchy Fritos. Macho Nachos are as loaded as you can get and deliciously messy and satisfying.

Hours

(Closed Sunday)
Mon. – Sat. . . . . 11 am – 10 pm

Cost

$3.50 - 6

Directions

From downtown, take San Pedro Street north to Hildebrand. Go left and continue to Blanco and go left again. Will be on Blanco and Hollywood Streets.

Where To Eat?

DICK'S LAST RESORT ON THE RIVER WALK

406 Navarro
San Antonio 78205
210-224-0026

American

Dick's on the River Walk is family fun during the day, but more adult oriented at night (no kids or teens are allowed after 9 pm, so plan accordingly). You'll get lots of good-natured ribbing as you snack on catfish, shrimp, and steak. A wide assortment of kids' plates offer everything from burgers to corn dogs and ribs.

Hours

Daily .... 11 am – 2 pm

Cost

Lunch $4-6
Dinner $10-18

Directions

Located on the River Walk under the Navarro Bridge, across from Planet Hollywood.

Where To Eat?

EL MIRADOR RESTAURANT

722 S. St. Mary's
San Antonio 78205
210-225-9444

Mexican

One of San Antonio's most beloved restaurants, El Mirador is everything you'd want in an established Tex-Mex restaurant—modestly priced, delicious food in a comfortable atmosphere. Soups, including Caldo Xochitl, are El Mirador's specialty, but puffy tacos, enchiladas, and chalupas compuestas are just as memorable. Prices and menu offerings are slightly more upscale at dinner.

Hours

Sunday .... 9 am – 3 pm

Breakfast

Mon. – Sat. .... 6:30 am – 11 am

Lunch

Mon. – Sat. .... 11 am – 3 pm

Dinner

Tues. – Thurs. .... 5 pm – 9 pm
Fri. and Sat. .... 5 pm – 10 pm

Cost

Lunch .... $3.95 - $7
Dinner .... $5.95 - $17

Directions

On the corner of S. St. Mary's
and Durango Streets.

Where To Eat?

GOLDEN WOK CHINESE RESTAURANT

8822 Wurzbach Road
San Antonio
210-615-8282

Chinese

If your kids have never had dim sum, this is the place to take them. On Saturdays and Sundays from 11:30 a.m.-1:30 p.m., carts piled high with steamer trays are rolled around the restaurant. When they stop at your table, you pick and choose at will from such items as shrimp dumplings and sweet rice tied in banana leaves. The earlier you come, the better the selection—some 20-25 items most days.

Hours

Mon. – Sat. . . . . 11 am – 10 pm

Cost

$5.95-22

Directions

From downtown, take I-10 West and exit Wurzbach. Go left. Will be 3 or 4 blocks down on the left.

Where To Eat?

GUENTHER HOUSE RESTAURANT

205 E. Guenther
San Antonio 78204
210-227-1061

American

Located in the King William area and part of the century-old Pioneer Flour Mill, Guenther House is the perfect place to enjoy a leisurely breakfast away from the rush of downtown.

Towering waffles are an excellent choice, as are the breakfast tacos and any of the fresh-baked goods.

Be sure to visit the accompanying store where you can purchase top-quality foodstuffs to recreate your own Guenther House specialties at home.

Hours

Mon. – Sat. .... 7 am – 3 pm
Sunday .... 8 am – 2 pm

Cost

$2.25- 6.95

Directions

Located next to the King William District. Take S. Alamo south of downtown and go right on E. Guenther.

Where To Eat?

GREY MOSS INN
19010 Scenic Loop Road
San Antonio
210-695-8301

Steaks

For 63 years, the Grey Moss Inn has been serving its famous steaks (cooked over a well in the courtyard) in a Hill Country setting that originally was a getaway from the heat of the city. The drive there is romantic—albeit dark and a bit winding.

Jalapeno- and bacon-stuffed twice-baked potatoes are tops, as is the signature squash casserole, served at the restaurant since it opened. Kids will be fascinated by the candles that flicker at the tables. With their waxy build-up, the candles look like they've been burning since the restaurant's opening in the '20s.

Hours
Mon. – Sat. ....5 pm – 10 pm

Cost
$16.95-40

Directions

From downtown, take I-10 West to 1604 and go west. Exit Babcock and go right for 6 miles, until it deadends. Go left on Scenic Loop Road and travel 2.5 miles. Will be on the left.

Where To Eat?

HARD ROCK CAFÉ OF SAN ANTONIO-RIVER WALK

111 W. Crockett Street
San Antonio 78205
210-224-7625

American

If two outfits that Madonna wore on stage don't interest you, maybe Eddie Van Halen's guitar will. Besides plenty of Hollywood memorabilia (including a stained-glass-window tribute to three stars from Texas), kids have plenty to choose from on their own menus, including macaroni and cheese, hot dogs, and hamburgers.

Adults can order from a wide selection of salads, sandwiches, and pasta or pick the popular rib and chicken combo platter. Oversized banana splits and chocolate chip cookie pie are great desserts for sharing.

Hours

Sun. – Thur. . . . . 11 am – 11 pm
Fri. – Sat. . . . . 11 am – Mid.

Cost

$5.95-18.95

Directions

Located at Crocket and Presa.

Where To Eat?

LA FOGATA

2427 Vance Jackson
San Antonio 78213
210-340-1337

Mexican

For 20 years, La Fogata has set the standard for Mexican dining in San Antonio. Eat outdoors in one of the city's loveliest alfresco settings or inside in cool comfort. Rajas con crema and quesadillas de hongos stuffed with white Mexican cheese and mushrooms are blissful, as are the green enchiladas.

The smoky, roasted salsa is available for take-home. Trust us—you'll want to.

Hours

Sat. and Sun Breakfast. . . . . 8 am – 11 am
Mon. – Fri. . . . . 11 am – 10 pm
Saturday . . . . 11 am – 11 pm
Sunday . . . . 11 am – 10 pm

Cost

$5.75-19.95

Directions

From downtown, take I-10 West and exit Vance Jackson. Go right. Will be on the left approximately 1 mile down.

Where To Eat?

LIBERTY BAR
328 E. Josephine St.
San Antonio 78215
210-227-1187

American

Don't be frightened, but this building tilts noticeably to the east. Not to fear, however—San Antonians have been safely dining there for years.

The eclectic, slightly upscale, somewhat Southern menu has something to please nearly everyone. Mexican-inspired entrees are especially satisfying, as is the restaurant's famous decadent chocolate cake.

Hours
Mon. – Thur. . . . . . . 11:30 am – 10:30 pm
Fri. – Sat. . . . . 11:30 am – Midnight
Sunday . . . . 10:30 am – 10:30 pm

Cost
$6.75 – 18.95

Directions
From downtown, take 281 North and exit Josephine. Will be on the corner. Or take Braodway north of downtown and go left on Josephine. Will be on the left.

Where To Eat?

MAGIC TIME MACHINE

902 Northeast Loop 410
San Antonio
210-828-1470

Steaks

As much entertainment as restaurant, Magic Time Machine entertains the young and the young at heart. A crazy cast of costumed characters serve your meals and create a magical mood with their jokes, songs, and friendly banter.

Kids will love the real '53 MG roadster that's been gutted and serves as a soup and salad bar. Parents will enjoy the fact that someone is giving them a break and doing some of the entertaining.

Hours

Daily .... 5:30 pm – 10 pm

Cost

$10-22

Directions

From downtown, take 281 North. Go east on 410 and exit Broadway. Pass Broadway. Will be on the right.

Where To Eat?

MI TIERRA CAFE AND BAKERY

218 Produce Row (in El Mercado)
San Antonio
210-225-1262

Mexican

Twenty-four hours a day, 365 days a year, Mi Tierra turns out its Mexican specialties. We find it most satisfying late at night, when other restaurants have long since closed their doors.

Caldo del Mercado is popular, as are the chiles rellenos and chalupas. But for sheer gluttony, try the Special Mexican Dinner—taco, tamale, cheese enchilada, chile con queso, guacamole, rice, beans, and flour tortillas.

An accompanying bakery counter sells fresh Mexican breads, cookies, and candies.

Hours

24 hours, year-round

Cost

$5-16

Directions

Located in Market Square, at I-35 and Commerce.

Where To Eat?

OLD SAN FRANCISCO STEAKHOUSE

10223 Sahara
San Antonio
210-342-2321

Steaks/Seafood

When you make reservations at this Gay '90s theme restaurant, request "The Swing Room" where the girl on the red velvet swing pumps herself to dizzying heights, ultimately ringing a bell on the 30-foot ceiling with her foot. Kids are allowed to take a (much-tamer) swing ride.

Diners start their meal with an oversized block of Swiss cheese and fresh-baked bread. Prime rib is good, as is the fish and chicken. A separate children's menu with prices starting at $3.50 is available.

Hours

Mon. – Thurs. . . . . .5 pm – 10 pm
Fri. – Sat. . . . . .5 pm – 11 pm
Sunday . . . . .4 pm – 11 pm

Cost

$16.95 - 36

Directions

Located 15 minutes from downtown. Take 281 North to the 410 Loop and go west. Exit San Pedro and travel north approximately 1 mile to Sahara. Go right. Will be on the right.

Where To Eat?

PALOMA BLANCA

5148 Broadway
San Antonio
210-822-6151

Mexican

One of San Antonio's newest, Paloma Blanca offers a memorable taste experience at modest prices.

Two varieties of salsa are among the best in the city, as are the homemade corn and flour tortillas. Order the soup, enchiladas, or chicken specialties with confidence. Homemade *tres leches* cake (soaked with three milks for an almost cheesecake-like consistency) is legendary.

Hours

Tues. – Thurs. . . . . 10:45 am – 10 pm
Fri. – Sat. . . . . 10:45 am – 10:30 pm
Saturday (breakfast) . . . . . . 8 am – 11 am

Cost

$5.25 – 10.95

Directions

Take Broadway north of downtown. Will be 3 stop signs past Hildebrand on the right.

Where To Eat?

PLANET HOLLYWOOD ON THE RIVER WALK

245 E. Commerce, Suite 100
San Antonio 78205
210-212-7827

American

Gift boxes and luggage from the movie *Titanic*. The alligator from *Ace Ventura: When Nature Calls*. A 10-foot teddy bear from *The Incredible Shrinking Woman*. With this and more, kids won't be bored here.

From a $5.95 special menu (including soft drink or milk), kids can choose from Chicken Crunch (chicken tenders coated with Cap'n Crunch cereal and corn flakes), pizza, or burgers. Adults may find the L.A. lasagna more to their liking. Both will go for the chocolate cake with dark and white chocolate ice creams.

Hours

Daily .... 11 am – 11 pm

Cost

$12.50 – 17.95

Directions

On the corner of Commerce and Navarro. Also has an entrance on the River Walk.

Where To Eat?

RIO RIO CANTINA ON THE RIVER WALK

421 E. Commerce
San Antonio 78205
210-226-8462

Mexican

Located one level up from the river, Rio Rio offers a lush view of River Walk activity in a cool, comfy atmosphere. Portions are oversized, so order carefully.

Rio Rio Enchiladas are a good pick, as are the appetizer quesadillas, which are more than enough for a kid's meal for sharing. Salsa is top-notch and free-flowing.

Hours

Daily .... 11 am – 10 pm to 10:30 pm

Cost

$6.95 – 13.95

Directions

On the Riverwalk. On the corner of Losoya and Commerce Streets.

Where To Eat?

RUDY'S COUNTRY STORE AND BBQ

24152 I-10 West
Leon Springs 78257
210-698-2141
and
10623 Westover Hills Blvd.
San Antonio
210-520-5552

Barbecue

You'll find lots of kid-pleasing food at either of these two locations (Leon Springs is the original), but there's plenty to make adults happy, too, including mouth-watering pork ribs, tenderloin, and brisket.

Grab a soft drink from icy troughs, then prepare to stand in line a while, as these are popular places. Regulars know to order some of Rudy's creamed corn on the side and to grab an extra bottle or two of barbecue sauce to take home with them.

Hours

Mon.–Thur. .... 10 am – 10 pm
Fri.- Sun. .... 10 am – 11 pm

Cost

$2 - 10.95

Directions

For the restaurant in Leon Springs coming from downtown, take I-10 West and exit 551 (Leon Springs). Will be on the right on the access road.

The San Antonio reataurant is located at 151 (Raymond Stotzer Freeway) and Westover Hills, across the street from the entrance to Sea World.

Where To Eat?

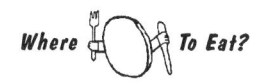

SCHILO'S DELICATESSEN

428 E. Commerce
San Antonio 78205
210-223-6692

Delicatessen

For 80-plus years, this downtown institution (near the River Walk, one level up) has been producing such specialties as split pea soup, chicken and dumplings and deli sandwiches. But it's their homemade root-beer served in frosty mugs that is most noteworthy. You'll never want to go back to the bottled kind after you taste the real stuff. (One free refill is included in the price—you'll want to take it.)

Hours

Mon. – Sat. . . . . 7 am – 8:30 pm

Cost

$5 - 9

Directions

Downtown at E. Commerce near the River Walk, between Presa and Navarro Streets.

Where To Eat?

SEA ISLAND SHRIMP HOUSE

5959 Northwest Loop 410, San Antonio 78238
210-520-3033

322 W. Rector, San Antonio
210-342-7771

4323 Amerisuites Dr., San Antonio 78230
210-558-8989

Seafood

So busy are these restaurants during rush hours that you get two numbers—one for a table, then one for your order. Not to worry. The system works well at this casual restaurant, waits are short, and the reasonably priced food is worth it.

Fried shrimp and fish are stellar. Cole slaw and hush puppies accompany beautifully. Gumbo is a must-have.

Hours

Mon. – Sat. . . . . 10:15 am – 9:30 pm
Sunday . . . . 10:15 am – 8:30 pm

Cost

$6-12

Directions from downtown

For Northwest Loop 410, take 281 North to 410 West and exit Exchange Parkway. Will be .5 mile on the right.

For Rector, take 281 North to 410 West and exit San Pedro Ave., go south. Turn left on W. Rector. On the immediate right behind the mall.

For Amerisuites, take I-10 W, exit Huebner Road. Stay on the access road. On your right before Huebner.

Where To Eat?

TOWER OF THE AMERICAS

222 HemisFair Park
San Antonio 78205
210-223-3101

American

This revolving restaurant atop the Tower of the Americas was part of HemisFair '68. Thirty years later, it's still revolving (one revolution per hour) and serving customers a spectacular view of all parts of the city.

Steak and seafood top the list. Kids have their own reasonably priced menu with their choice of nachos, fried shrimp, chicken fingers, and burgers.

Hours

Lunch

Mon. – Fri. . . . . 11 am – 2 pm
Sat. – Sun. . . . . 11 am – 2:30 pm

Dinner

Sun. – Thur. . . . . 5:30 pm – 10 pm
Fri. – Sun. . . . . 5:30 pm – 10:30 pm

Cost

$12 -30

Directions

Located downtown on Bowie, between Market and Durango Streets.

Where To Eat?

ZUNI GRILL
511 River Walk
210-227-0864

American

Besides good food, Zuni Grill has another way of making parents happy. When you come in late in the evening with small kids that are getting tired and grumpy, Zuni's waitstaff often will bring complimentary bowls of chopped fruit or flour tortillas for snacking along with the more adult chips and salsa. Anything to please is their motto. Adults will especially appreciate this gesture.

Hours

Daily . . . . 8 am – 10 pm

Cost
$9.95-20

Directions

At Losoya and Crocket. On the River Walk, two restaurants from the Hyatt Regency.

Where To Eat?

Locations

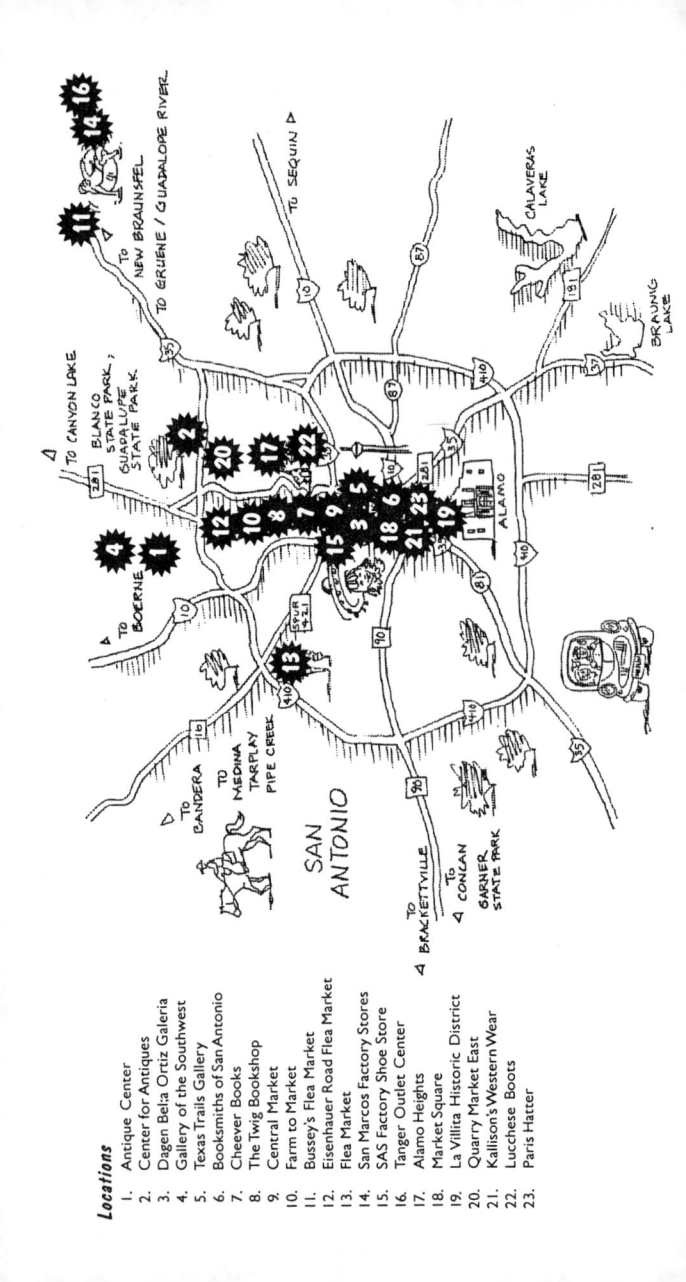

1. Antique Center
2. Center for Antiques
3. Dagen Bela Ortiz Galeria
4. Gallery of the Southwest
5. Texas Trails Gallery
6. Booksmiths of San Antonio
7. Cheever Books
8. The Twig Bookshop
9. Central Market
10. Farm to Market
11. Bussey's Flea Market
12. Eisenhauer Road Flea Market
13. Flea Market
14. San Marcos Factory Stores
15. SAS Factory Shoe Store
16. Tanger Outlet Center
17. Alamo Heights
18. Market Square
19. La Villita Historic District
20. Quarry Market East
21. Kallison's Western Wear
22. Lucchese Boots
23. Paris Hatter

Chapter 8
UNIQUE PLACES TO SHOP

Antique Shops 164
    Antique Center
    Center for Antiques
Art Gallereis 165
    Dagen Bel;a Ortiz Galeria
    Gallery of the Southwest
    Texas Trails Gallery
Bookstores 166
    Booksmiths of San Antonio
    Cheever Books
    The Twig Bookshop
Food Markets 167
    Central Market
    Farm to Market
Flea Markets 168
    Bussey's Flea Market
    Eisenhauer Road Flea Market
    Flea Market
Outlet Stores 169
    San Marcos Factory Stores
    SAS Factory Shoe Store
    Tanger Outlet Center
Unique Places To Shop 170
    Alamo Heights
    Market Square
    La Villita Historic District
    Quarry Market East
Unique Shops 171
    Kallison's Western Wear
    Lucchese Boots
    Paris Hatter

Unique Places to Shop

ANTIQUE SHOPS

Antique Center
11345 West Ave.
San Antonio 78213
210-344-4131

Find a little of everything at this antique center, one of the largest antique stores away from the downtown area. Specialty items include juke boxes, Coca-Cola machines, glass, and signs. Go left two blocks from Blanco Road on West Street.

Mon. – Sat. .... 10am – 6pm
Sun. .... noon – 5pm

Center for Antiques
8505 Broadway (outside Loop 410)
San Antonio 78217
210-804-6300

Over 115 dealers fill this center with every kind of antique imaginable. One of the largest antique dealers in San Antonio.

Mon. – Fri. .... 10 am – 6pm
Sat. .... 10 am – 6pm
Sun. .... noon – 5pm

Unique Places to Shop

ART GALLERIES

The Dagen Bela Ortiz Galeria
102 Concho (Market Square)
San Antonio 78207
210-225-0731

Shop at one of the most unique galleries in San Antonio, featuring works of local Hispanic artists and artists from Mexico. The gallery displays custom jewelry, pottery, bronze sculptures, Mexican folk art, and other fascinating art pieces.

Weekdays . . . . 10 am – 5:30 pm
Weekends . . . . open until 8 pm

Gallery of the Southwest
13485 Blanco (and Bitters Roads)
San Antonio 78231
210-493-3344

Every things in this store is Southwestern. Shop for items from the Hopi, Navaho, and Zuni Indians: rugs, pottery, paintings, watercolors, and oils. The shop offers collectibles and interesting pawn pieces.

Tues. – Sat. 10 am – 5pm

Texas Trails Gallery
245 Losoya (and Commerce Streets)
San Antonio 78205
210-224-7865

Visit a traditional gallery with a large range of subjects and styles.

Mon. – Sat. 10 am – 6pm
Sun. . . . . 10 am – 5pm

Unique Places to Shop

BOOKSTORES

Booksmiths of San Antonio
209 Alamo Plaza
San Antonio 78205
210-271-9177

This family-owned store specializes in regional books—from southwestern cookbooks to books on the Alamo. Downstairs you'll find literature for kids. Stop at their deli for tasty pastries, soups, and sandwiches. Located across from the Alamo.

Cheever Books
140 Carnahan St.
San Antonio 78209
210-824-2665

Located in the Alamo Heights area across from the Witte Museum, this bookstore carries a huge selection of used books—many rare. Take Broadway past 35N (near Brachenridge Park) to Carnahan St. and go right.

Mon.-Sat. .... 10 am – 8 pm
Sun. .... noon – 8 pm

The Twig Bookshop
5005 Broadway
Alamo Heights 78209
800-729-8944 • 210-826-6411

Located in the delightful Alamo Heights area minutes from downtown San Antonio, the Twig Bookshop carries a nice selection of children's literature, fiction, and Texana.

Unique Places to Shop

FOOD MARKETS

Central Market
4821 Broadway (at Hildebrand)
Alamo Heights 78209
210-368-8600

See what's in store at H.E.B.'s grandest 2-story grocery market, featuring over 4000 specialty items. Chefs prepare 80 different dishes ready for you to take home. You'll find natural foods, fresh seafood, a made-from-scratch bakery, a huge floral department, a catering service, a gift gallery, a cooking school, and much more.

Opens daily .... 7 am – 10 pm

Farm to Market
1133 Austin Highway (368)
San Antonio 78209
210-822-4450

Buy Texas produce fresh from the farm with lots of other unique imported and specialty items. Choose from 20 different olive oils or from a large variety of dried pastas. The deli offers 15-20 salads and soups—from chicken noodle to oriental varieties—and the butcher shop features fresh meats and seafood.

Take Broadway north of downtown. Take Austin Highway to the northeast. Will be on the left.

Opens daily .... 8:30 am – 7 pm

Unique Places to Shop

FLEA MARKETS

Bussey's Flea Market
18738 I-35 North
San Antonio
210-651-6830

Opens Saturdays and Sundays 7 am – 5:30 pm, with 20 acres of indoor and outdoor vendors. Rent a booth or come to browse. You'll find everything imaginable, from antiques, tools, and crafts, to garage sale and import items. Located about 30 minutes from downtown. Worth the drive.

Eisenhauer Road Flea Market
3903 Eisenhauer Road
San Antonio 78218
210-653-7592

An indoor air-conditioned market that features all kinds of items, used and new. Also offers barbecue food and snack bars. Take Broadway north of downtown and continue to the right (northeast) from Austin Parkway. Turn right on Eisenhauer.

Opens Wed. – Fri. . . . . noon – 7pm
Sat. – Sun. 9am – 7pm

Flea Market
12280 Highway 16 South (1 mile south of Loop 410)
San Antonio
210-624-2666

A huge authentic Mexican market filled with all kinds of things: clothes, crafts, fruits, vegetables, and foods like homemade tamales and tortillas. Festive atmosphere with live music.

Sat. and Sun. . . . . 10 am – 6 pm.

Unique Places to Shop

OUTLET STORES

San Marcos Factory Stores
3939 I-35 South (Exit 200), San Marcos 78666
800-628-9465 • 512-396-7183

Take 25-75% off at the largest factory outlet in Texas, with over 119 stores. Many upscale name brands stores, such as Donna Karan, Polo Ralph Lauren, and Ann Taylor. Just 45 min. from San Antonio.

Mon. – Sat. . . . . 10 am – 9 pm
Sun. . . . . 11 am – 6 pm

SAS Factory Shoe Store
101 N. Laredo Highway (at Zaramore)
San Antonio 78207
210-924-6507

San Antonio manufactured leather shoes with small, hardly-noticeable defects at great savings. Save $20-30 on a pair of shoes. Buy shoes for the whole family—infants to adults—along with purses and belts.

Mon. – Fri. . . . . 10 am – 9 pm
Sun. . . . . 9 am – 5 pm

Tanger Outlet Center
4015 I-35 South (Exit 200), San Marcos 78666
800-408-8424

Across the street from the San Marcos Factory Stores, shop at one of the largest Tanger Outlet Centers. Over 50 stores with popular name brands such as Reebok, Disney, Dansk, Liz Claiborne, Claiborne for Men, Elizabeth, Kitchen Collection, Polo Jean Co. and much more. You'll find yourself in shopper's heaven.

Mon. – Sat. . . . . 9 am – 9 pm
Sun. . . . . 11 am – 6 pm

UNIQUE PLACES TO SHOP

Alamo Heights
Broadway
San Antonio

This upscale suburban area, with its array of classy shops along Broadway, makes for a fun afternoon. Two small interesting shopping areas include the Lincoln Heights (Broadway and Basse) and The Collection at Broadway and Sunset). Shop hours vary.

Market Square
514 W. Commerce Street, San Antonio 78207
210-207-8600

Any tourist wanting to see San Antonio must visit Market Square. Eat great Tex-Mex food, listen to mariachis, and shop at authentic shops. Festivals frequently take place in the open plazas.

Open daily 10 am to 5 pm (summer to 8 pm)

La Villita Historic District
418 Villita Street, San Antonio • 210-207-8610

What was the first original settlement is now a hot spot for art galleries. You'll find unique little shops. Buy tickets here for the Arneson Theater or attend one of Fiesta's biggest events, *A Night in Old San Antonio* in April.

Open daily .... 10 am – 5 pm

Quarry Market East
Hwy 281 North (at E. Basse Road), San Antonio

It's the giant smokestacks in the center of the complex—one of San Antonio's oldest landmarks—that first catch your attention. Shop at this unique Post-Industrial designed shopping center that now fills the old rock-crushing Alamo Cement Plant. Shops include Borders Books, Canyon Café, Joe's Crab Shack, Paesano's, Whole Foods Market, and more. Shop hours vary.

Unique Places to Shop

UNIQUE SHOPS

Kallison's Western Wear

123 S. Flores St. (at Dolorosa St.)
San Antonio 78204
210-222-1364

Kallison is the place for western wear—San Antonio's oldest. Shop here for hats, shirts, jeans, boots.
Open Mon. – Sat. .... 10 am – 6 pm.

Lucchese Boots

4025 Broadway (south of Hildebrand)
San Antonio 78209
210-828-9419

An immigrant from Italy, Sam Lucchese, brought to San Antonio the boot-making skills that produced the best in western boots. Now a corporation, see some of the finest boots, many from exotic hides.
Open daily .... 10 am – 6 pm

Paris Hatter

119 Broadway (downtown)
San Antonio 78205
210-223-3453

One of the most unique shops to San Antonio, the Paris Hatter has custom fitted western hats for nearly a century to many a well-known celebrity. One of the largest western hat stores in the country.
Open daily .... 9 am – 6 pm

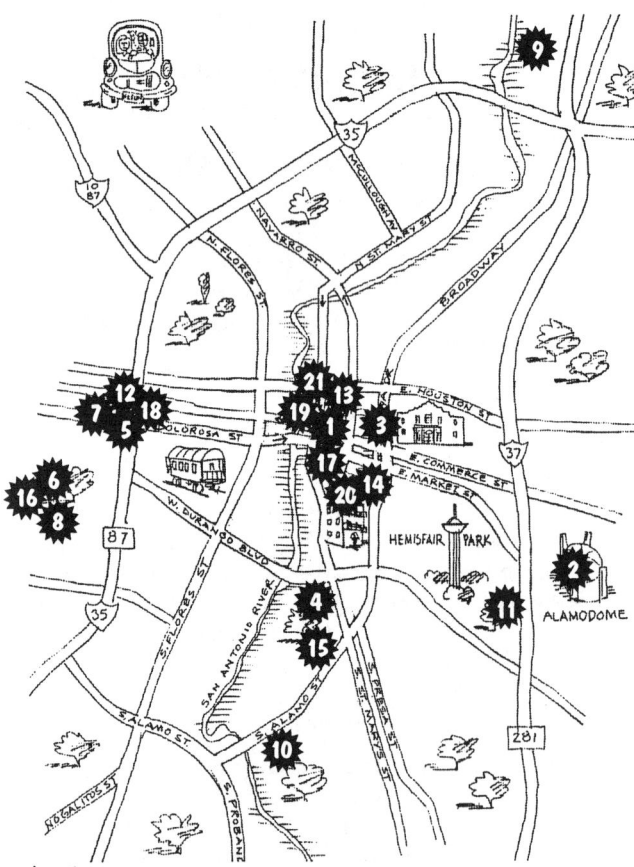

Locations

1. Annual Miller Lite River Walk Mud Festival and Arts and Crafts Show
2. San Antonio Stock Show and Rodeo
3. Dyeing O' the River Green Parade and Irish Show
4. Fiesta San Antonio
5. Cinco De Mayo Celebration
6. Annual Tejano Conjunto Festival en San Antonio
7. The Return of the Chili Queens
8. San Antonio CineFestival
9. Shakespeare in the Park
10. Contemporary Art Month
11. Texas Folklife Festival
12. Fiestas Patria
13. Annual Jazz'SAlive
14. Big Country River Festival
15. Oktoberfest San Antonio
16. Inter-American Bookfair and Literary Festival
17. Lighting Ceremony and River Walk Holiday Parade
18. Feria de Santa Cecilia and Fiestas Navidenas
19. Rivercenter Christmas Pageant
20. Fiesta de las Luminarias
21. Las Posadas

Chapter 9
ANNUAL EVENTS

January	Annual Miller Lite River Walk Mud Festival and Arts and Crafts Show ...	174
February	San Antonio Stock Show and Rodeo .	174
March	Dyeing O' the River Green Parade and Irish Show	174
April	Fiesta San Antonio	175
May	Cinco De Mayo Celebration	175
	Annual Tejano Conjunto Festival en San Antonio..........	175
	The Return of the Chili Queens	176
June	San Antonio CineFestival.........	176
	Shakespeare in the Park..........	176
July	Contemporary Art Month	177
August	Texas Folklife Festival	177
September	Fiestas Patria	177
	Annual Jazz'SAlive..............	177
	Big Country River Festival........	178
October	Oktoberfest San Antonio	178
	Inter-American Bookfair and Literary Festival	178
November	Lighting Ceremony and River Walk Holiday Parade	178
	Feria de Santa Cecilia and Fiestas Navidenas	179
December	Rivercenter Christmas Pageant	179
	Fiesta de las Luminarias	179
	Las Posadas..................	179

Watch For These   *Annual Events*

January

Annual Miller Lite River Walk Mud Festival & Arts and Crafts Show
210-227-4262

This annual event coincides with the draining of the river for maintenance. An elected mud king and queen reign over the Mud Pie Ball and the Mud Parade. Arts and crafts line the River Walk. On weekdays, times are from 5-9 pm; weekends, 10 am-10 pm. Admission is free.

February

San Antonio Stock Show and Rodeo
210-225-5851

The Stock Show and Rodeo begins each year with a Cowboy Breakfast that feeds 55,000 people fresh breakfast tacos and other tasty foods at the Central Park Mall. Twenty PRCA (Professional Rodeo Cowboy Association) rodeos, held at the Freemen Coliseum, feature big-name country, Tejano, and rock n' roll artists. Events include the Family Fair, shopping, and the livestock shows. Admission charged.

March

Dyeing O' the River Green Parade and Irish Show
210-497-8435

The San Antonio River becomes a River Shannon when 30 pounds of environmentally safe dye are dumped into it. A parade begins at La Mansion del Rio Hotel and proceeds to the Arneson Theater. More Irish entertainment takes place at the Arneson Theater. Free.

Watch For These   *Annual Events*

April

Fiesta San Antonio
210-227-5191

This 10-day citywide celebration is San Antonio's largest event, hosting 3.5 million visitors. The event includes carnivals, sports events, fireworks, musical entertainment, ethnic feasts, art exhibits, and parades—on the street and on the river. The festival, begun in 1891, honors Texas heroes and San Antonio's rich cultural heritage. It now features over 150 events such as Nights in Old San Antonio with 15 areas of food and entertainment that represent San Antonio's many ethnic influences (admission charged). The King William Fair features a parade, arts and crafts, musical entertainment, food, drinks, and more (free admission).

May

Cinco de Mayo Celebration
210-207-8600

Market Square celebrates the Battle of Pueblo, fought between the Mexican and the French forces that led to Mexico's independence. Sponsored by the Mexican American Cultural Center, the event is held on the closest weekend to the fifth of May with music, food, arts, and crafts. Free admission.

Annual Tejano Conjunto Festival en San Antonio
210-271-3151

Over 40,000 people attend the Guadalupe Cultural Arts Center's 6-day music festival, featuring 42 hours of live performances—with some of the best Tejano and conjunto musical groups in the country.

Watch For These   *Annual Events*

Activities include a national poster contest, exhibits, and inductees into the Conjunto Music Hall of Fame. Enjoy accordion student recitals, food booths, games, and dancing. Events are held at Rose Dale Park at 340 Dartmouth Street and at the Guadalupe Theater. Admissions are good for an entire day, $6-8.

The Return of the Chili Queens
210-207-8600

Market Square relives the days of the famous Chili Queens as chili and other Mexican foods are served from tables set out on the open plazas, as it was in days past. Admission is free.

June

San Antonio CineFestival
210-271-3151

Attend the oldest and largest Chicano and Latino film festival in the country—a huge filmmaker's conference. This five-day event takes place at the Guadalupe Cultural Arts Center's theater at different times of the year (June 16-20, 1999). Competitions include documentary, fiction, and experimental films. Admission to a screening is $6-8. Some screenings are free. One, in particular, caters to children. Call for more details.

Shakespeare in the Park
210-226-2891

Arts! San Antonio features the best of Shakespeare, outdoors under the stars, at the San Antonio Botanical Gardens. Free: donations accepted.

Watch For These   *Annual Events*

July

Contemporary Art Month
210-227-6960

San Antonio focuses on its art community with over 70 events that involve more than 700 artists, performers, and musicians. Sponsored by the Blue Star Arts Complex.

August

Texas Folklife Festival
210-558-2300

Each year the Institute of Texas Cultures celebrates the diversity of our state's ethnic and cultural groups with a festival that includes stories, crafts, music, dance, and foods. Admission charged.

September

Fiestas Patrias
210-207-8600

Market Square celebrates Diez y Seis, Mexico's independence from Spain, with entertainment and food. Sponsored by the Ladies LULAC Council 648. Free admission.

Annual Jazz'SAlive
210-207-8486

A jazz festival with bands from New Orleans and San Antonio, held at Travis Park and sponsored by the San Antonio Parks Foundation and San Antonio Parks and Recreation Department. Enjoy arts, crafts, and food booths. Free admission.

Watch For These   *Annual Events*

Big Country River Festival
210-227-4262

Enjoy this music festival that includes an arts and crafts show. Held one weekend in late September at the River Walk's Arneson River Theater. Free admission.

October
Oktoberfest San Antonio
210-222-1521

Enjoy authentic German food and drink at the Beethoven Haus and Gardens in the Historic King William District. Musical groups come from Munich, Germany, to entertain. Admission charged.

Inter-American Bookfair and Literary Festival
210-271-3151

The Guadalupe Cultural Arts Center's theater hosts the annual Inter-American Bookfair and Literary Festival. Focusing on Chicano, Latino, and Native American writers, the festival features poetry and fiction readings, workshops, and book exhibits. Daytime events are free. Admission is charged for evening activities, $6-8. Opens on a Wednesday and runs through Saturday each October.

November
Lighting Ceremony and River Walk Holiday Parade
210-227-4262

Held the Friday after Thanksgiving at 7 pm. Watch as over 100,000 lights switch on and light up the River Walk for the holidays. Activities include a parade of decorated boats that includes Santa's debut. Admission charge.

Watch For These   *Annual Events*

Feria de Santa Cecilia & Fiestas Navidenas
210-207-8600

See the lighting of Market Square that marks the beginning of the holiday season. Events include the Blessing of Animals and a visit from Pancho Claus. Free admission.

December

Rivercenter Christmas Pageant
210-225-0000

River barges portray the Christmas story as they float into the Rivercenter Mall's lagoon and unfold a classic nativity scene. Admission is charged for reserved seating. Open seating is free.

Fiesta de las Luminarias
210-227-4262

Candles, more than 2500 luminarias, line the walkways along the River Walk to symbolically light for the Holy Family. Sponsored by the Paseo del Rio Association. Free.

Las Posadas
210-224-6163

The Conservation Society presents an annual Spanish Christmas tradition of Joseph and Mary seeking a room at an inn—a religious drama from Mexico brought here by Franciscan friars in the 16th century. Children costumed as Joseph and Mary lead the candle-bearing procession that includes angels, shepherds, mariachis, and a choir. The procession begins at Crockett Street in front of the La Mansion del Rio Hotel. The public may join the procession or watch from the River Walk or near the Arneson River Theater. Free admission.

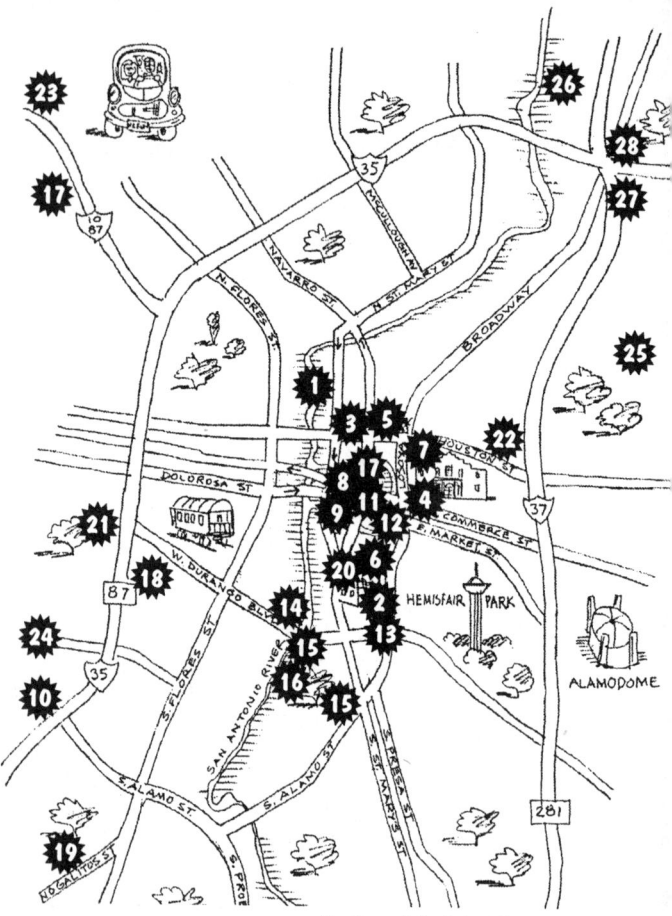

Locations

1. Adam's Mark Hotel River Walk
2. Fairmount Hotel
3. Historic Camberley Gunter Hotel
4. Historic Menger Hotel
5. Historic Crown Plaza St. Anthony
6. Hilton Palacio del Rio
7. Holiday Inn Crocket Hotel
8. Holiday Inn River Walk
9. Homewood Suites River Walk
10. Hyatt Regency Hill Country Resort
11. La Mansion del Rio
12. Marriotts Riverwalk / Rivercenter
13. Plaza San Antonio
14. Riverwalk Inn Bed and Breakfast
15. Noble Inn
16. Oge House on the River Walk
17. Days Inn and Suites Fiesta Park
18. Fairfield Inn by Marriott
19. Hampton Inn Sea World
20. Holiday Inn Express
21. Radisson Market Square
22. Residence Inn Alamo Plaza
23. Super 8 Motel Six Flags Fiesta Texas
24. Admiralty Park
25. Dixie Kampground
26. Creek Hollow RV Park
27. Hill Country RV Park
28. Maricopa Ranch resort

Chapter 10
WHERE TO STAY?

Swanky, Upscale, and Famous Hotels in San Antonio

- Adam's Mark Hotel River Walk............ 182
- Fairmount Hotel 182
- Historic Camberley Gunter Hotel 183
- Historic Menger Hotel 183
- Historic Crown Plaza St. Anthony 184
- Hilton Palacio del Rio 184
- Holiday Inn Crocket Hotel 185
- Holiday Inn River Walk 186
- Homewood Suites River Walk 186
- Hyatt Regency Hill Country Resort 187
- La Mansion del Rio 187
- Marriotts Riverwalk / Rivercenter 188
- Plaza San Antonio 188

Bed and Breakfast Inns

- Riverwalk Inn Bed and Breakfast 189
- Noble Inn............................ 190
- Oge House on the River Walk 191

Other Great Hotel and Motel Accommodations

- Days Inn and Suites Fiesta Park 192
- Fairfield Inn by Marriott 192
- Hampton Inn Sea World 192
- Holiday Inn Express.................... 192
- Radisson Market Square 192
- Residence Inn Alamo Plaza 192
- Super 8 Motel Six Flags Fiesta Texas....... 192

R.V. Parks and Camping

- Admiralty Park........................ 193
- Dixie Kampground 193
- Creek Hollow RV Park 193
- Hill Country RV Park................... 193
- Maricopa Ranch resort 193

Where To Stay?

SWANKY, UPSCALE, AND FAMOUS HOTELS

Adam's Mark Hotel RiverWalk

111 E. Pecan, 78205
800-444-2326 • 210-354-2800

The Adam's Mark Hotel offers 410 luxurious rooms and 4 suites. Amenities include in-room movies, two phone lines per room, an oversized working desk, a business center, an outdoor pool, a health club, a Jacuzzi, a gift shop, baby sitting, and laundry facilities. Their full service restaurant serves breakfast, lunch, and dinner.

Cost - $175-900

Directions - From I-35 exit Main Street and go south. Turn left on Pecan Street. The hotel will be on Soledad, between E. Martin and Pecan Streets.

Fairmount Hotel

401 S. Alamo, 78205
210-224-8800

The Fairmount Hotel sets a record in the Guinness Book of World Records. Its trek across town is recorded as "the heaviest building ever moved on wheels." At the same time, an excavation of its present location revealed many artifacts used during the Battle of the Alamo. The hotel now sits on a State Archaeological Landmark and displays the findings.

Built in 1906, it originated as a hotel for railway travelers. Now meticulously restored, this small red brick and limestone luxury hotel, with Italianate Victorian architecture, specializes in personal service. Enjoy staying in one of their plush 19 guestrooms or 17 suites. The hotel considers itself a "country-style bed and breakfast within the city limits."

Cost - $195-550

Directions - Across from the HemisFair Plaza.

Historic Camberley Gunter Hotel

205 E. Houston 78205
210-227-3241

Treat yourself any morning at Gunter Hotel's bakery and enjoy some of the finest baked goods in San Antonio. This classy hotel sits across the street from the Majestic Theatre and features lots of family amenities: a swimming pool, an exercise room, a gift shop, a barbershop, a child-sitting service, a full-service dining room, and a shoe shine. Note the Swiss-German décor and the art that hangs in the hotel, particularly the one over the staircase on the third floor—they're originals. For valet parking use the entrance on St. Mary's and Travis Streets. Conveniently located in downtown San Antonio.

Cost - $119-350

Directions - Corner of E. Houston and St. Mary's.

Historic Menger Hotel

204 Alamo 78205
800-345-9285 210-223-4361

Built in 1859 as the finest hotel west of the Mississippi, the Menger's history includes many famous people: Ulysses S. Grant, Robert E. Lee, Sarah Bernhardt, and Oscar Wilde. Still as charming today, the hotel offers a self-guided tour. See the ballroom, note the artwork, walk the hallways. Ask the front desk for a pamphlet.

Where To Stay?

Modern amenities at the Menger Hotel: an outdoor heated pool, a hot tub, a spa, an exercise room, a valet laundry, a limo service, a shopping arcade, and a gift shop.

Cost - $112-550

Directions - Between the Alamo and Rivercenter Mall.

Historic Crown Plaza St. Anthony
300 E. Travis 78205
800-277-6963 • 210-227-4392

Stay in a hotel designated a Texas and National Landmark. Built in 1909, the St. Anthony is known for elegance and old-world style. See many French Empire antiques and original oils and watercolors by such artists as Remington, Cartier, and DeYoung. The lobby features an eight-foot French chandelier, handpainted Mexican tiles, and priceless Chinese vases.

The St. Anthony is located across the street from historic Travis Park and one block from the River Walk. Walk to many of the attractions in downtown from the hotel. I truly enjoyed staying here.

Cost - $140-275

Directions - From I-37 exit Commerce Street and go left. Turn right on Navarro Street, then right on Travis Street. The hotel will be on the corner of Navarro and Travis Streets.

Hilton Palacio del Rio
200 S. Alamo 78205
800 Hiltons   210-222-1400

This 22-story hotel set a record, opening in only 202 days for the 1968 World's Fair. With aggressive planning, the hotel used precast concrete modules—500 furnished bedrooms, weighing 35 tons—all ready to hoist in to place. You'll enjoy staying at this 4-Diamond hotel located right on the River Walk. Best of all, children under 18 stay free with their parents or even grandparents. All rooms offer private balconies with a fantastic view. Other hotel features include an outdoor swimming pool (on the roof), a hot tub, a fitness room, a full-service business center, valet parking, and laundry facilities. Transportation to the airport leaves every 40 minutes for $6.

Cost - $201-775

Directions - Across from the entrance to HemisFair Park.

Holiday Inn Crockett Hotel
320 Bonham 78205
210-225-6500

History and location make the Crockett Hotel a novelty. Situated next to the Alamo, this 100-year-old 7-story hotel is located in in the historic part of downtown San Antonio. Guests easily walk to many of the attractions like the River Walk or the Rivercenter Mall. The décor includes a southwestern flavor with pine furnishings and artwork depicting regional history. The upper stories' view of downtown can't be beat. Enjoy the rooftop hot tub and the swimming pool. Compared to others downtown, the hotel is smaller and unpretentious, with 206 rooms.

Cost - $119-139

Directions - Next to the Alamo.

Where To Stay?

Holiday Inn River Walk

217 N. St. Mary's St. 78205
800-465-4329 • 210-224-2500

Kids under 12 eat free anytime at the Holiday Inn River Walk's restaurant, Fandangos. The hotel is located on the River Walk and conveniente to most of the downtown attractions. Family amenities include a game room, a swimming pool, an exercise room, a whirlpool, and a gift shop. Rooms feature king beds and extra work space. Suites offer refrigerators.

Cost - $125-275

Directions - From I-37 South, exit Commerce/Alamo. Turn right on Commerce, then right on Soledad, then left on Houston to N. St. Mary's.

Homewood Suites River Walk

432 West Market 78205
800-225-5466 • 210-222-1515

Homewood Suites—one of the best bets for any family wanting to visit San Antonio. Enjoy a view of the river with your complimentary continental breakfast that includes cereal, waffles, pancakes, bagels, fruit, juices, and more. Evenings include a 2-hour social featuring a complimentary light meal or snacks.

Suites come with 1 or 2 bedrooms, a living room, and a fully equipped kitchen with a microwave, a full refrigerator, a dishwasher, dining tables, plates, silverware, pots, and pans. Located within walking distance of most attractions.

Cost - $99-169 Suites

Directions - Located on Market and St. Mary's.

Hyatt Regency Hill Country Resort

9800 Hyatt Regency Dr. 78251
800-233-1234 • 210-647-1234

The Hyatt Regency Hill Country Resort is a 200-acre family retreat. Kids tube in their 950-foot Ramblin' River and splash in a shallow pool April through October, weather permitting. Camp Hyatt's crafts, hiking, and swimming, for kids while parents enjoy the adult amenities. Call and make reservations at least 72 hours in advance. The resort offers tennis, golf, an exercise room, a fitness center, a swimming pool, and 3 full restaurants. And there's more nearby: horseback riding, rock climbing, sailing, and fishing.

Suites come with one or two bedrooms. It is located minutes away from SeaWorld.

Cost - $255-660

Directions - Take I-10 West to 90 West to 151 West. Go approximately 15 minutes to the Hyatt Regency Hill Country Resort and go right.

La Mansion del Rio Hotel

112 College St. 78205
800-292-7300 • 210-225-2581

Stay where celebrities like to stay in San Antonio. Built in 1854 as a catholic boys' school it converted to a hotel in time for the World's Fair. Unique in its design, the hotel features an old-world Spanish courtyard. Considered a historic treasure, it is located on the River Walk and within walking distance of the Convention Center and the Alamo. Amenities include an attached parking garage, a ballroom, a gift shop, plush rooms, and great service.

Cost - $210-1900

Directions - Located at the corner of College Street and Navarro or St. Mary's Streets.

Marriotts Riverwalk/Rivercenter
101 Bowie St. 78205
800-228-9290 • 210-223-1000

Every tree along the River Walk lights up for the holidays. Get a spectacular view from your own balcony facing the river at the **Marriott Riverwalk Hotel**. Or simply watch the sun set. You'll find the best view in town from their rooms. Balconies come with chairs, tables, and room service.

Because the **Marriott Rivercenter** is connected with the Rivercenter Mall, enjoy shopping over at 100 stores. Other family amenities include babysitting, a fast-food court, indoor-outdoor swimming pools, a whirlpool, an executive health club, saunas, parking, a gift shop, and restaurants.

Cost - $209-900

Directions - (These Marriotts are located next to each other.) From 281, exit Commerce Street and go west 1 block. The hotels will be on the right.

Plaza San Antonio
555 S. Alamo St. 78205
210-229-1000

Imagine relaxing at a spacious resort hotel in busy downtown San Antonio. The Plaza San Antonio, the only downtown hotel with tennis courts, sits on 6 lush acres. See the free-roaming exotic birds: peacocks and Chinese pheasants. Enjoy the health club, the swimming pool, valet parking, and in-room service. Best of all, the hotel is located two blocks from the River Walk and three from the Alamo. Considered a world-class hotel, the Plaza San Antonio rates as "one of the top 25 in the country"— 4 Diamond, 4 Stars—with award-winning catering.

Cost - $199-370

Directions - On S. Alamo and E. Durango Streets, across the street from the HemisFair Park.

Where To Stay?

BED AND BREAKFAST INNS

Riverwalk Inn Bed and Breakfast

329 Old Guilbeau, 78204
800-254-4440
www.virtualcities.com

What happens when you reassemble log cabins from Tennessee along the River Walk? You get a lot of charm at this bed and breakfast inn. Five 19th-century log homes came to San Antonio from Tennessee—log by log. Enjoy sitting on the porch in a rocker or in front of the fireplace when it's cold out. Beds come with old-fashioned quilts and rooms with country antiques. Your stay includes a continental breakfast sitting at a rustic antique table. Every afternoon, a freshly baked snack awaits you as you come in from sightseeing. Believe me, when your vacation is over, you won't want to leave.

Cost

Rooms with river view

Weekdays $99-125
Weekends $110-175

Directions

From 281, exit Durango St./Alamo dome. Stay in the right-hand lane and turn right on Durango. Go .8 mile, crossing S. Alamo and S. St. Mary's Streets and turn right on Aubrey St. The inn will be on the corner of Aubrey and Guilbeau Streets.

Where To Stay?

Noble Inns

Jackson House
107 Madison 78204

Pancoast Carriage House
202 Washington Street
210-225-4045
www.nobleinns.com

Let the Noble Inns know and they will pick you up at the airport in their classic 1960 Rolls Royce Silver Cloud II. Stay in the heart of the King William District in 100-year-old Victorian homes meticulously restored and designated as historical landmarks. Choose between the Pancoast Carriage House and the Jackson House. Each offers fresh flowers, guest robes, linen, daily maid service, and more. Rooms come with Victorian antiques, fireplaces, private marble baths, and modern amenities such as phones, cable TV, air-conditioning, and dataports. The inns are conveniently located within walking distance of many downtown attractions.

Cost
$120-175

Directions

For the Jackson House, from Durango Street turn right on S. St. Mary's and turn right again on Madison Street. For the Pancoast Carriage, take Durango Street past S. St. Mary's and go left on Pancoast. The street forks, take Washington Avenue. The inn will be the first driveway on the left.

Where To Stay?

Oge House Inn on the River Walk
209 Washington Street, 78204
210-223-2353
www.ogeinn.com

The Oge House, a 19th-century mansion, is listed as a Texas Historical Landmark and on the National Register of Historic Places. Built in 1837 and once owned by Texas Ranger Louis Oge, the house now serves as a charming bed and breakfast inn in the King William Historical District. Each room and suite offers a private bath; most have fireplaces. Enjoy modern conveniences: telephones, cable TV, refrigerators. Eat breakfast either in the formal dining room or on the veranda. Catch the streetcar a few blocks away for all the attractions.

Cost
$145-205

Directions
From I-37, take the Durango/Alamodome exit and go left on Durango. Go through 4 stop lights and turn left after St. Mary's onto Pancoast Street. The Inn will be the 1st house on your right. Park behind the hedge.

Where To Stay?

OTHER GREAT HOTEL AND MOTEL ACCOMMODATIONS

Days Inn and Suites Fiesta Park
11790 I-10 West 78230
800-329-7466   210-692-7922

Fairfield Inn by Marriott
620 S. Santa Rosa 78204
800-228-2800   210-299-1000

Hampton Inn Sea World
4803 Manitou 78228
210-684-9966

Holiday Inn Express Hotel & Suites
524 S. St. Mary's 78205
800-969-3239   210-354-1333

Radisson Market Square
502 W. Durango 78207
210-224-7155

Residence Inn Alamo Plaza
425 Bonham 78205
800-331-3131   210-212-5555

Super 8 Motel Six Flags Fiesta Texas
5319 Casa Bella (I-10 West) 78249
800-800-8000   210-696-6916

Where To Stay?

RV PARKS AND CAMPING

Admiralty Park

1485 Ellison Dr., San Antonio, 78251 • 210-647-7878

Offers a free shuttle to SeaWorld, near Fiesta Texas. offers 240 concrete pads, a pool, a Jacuzzi, cable TV, free movies.

Dixie Kampground

1011 Gembler Rd., San Antonio 78219 • 210-337-6501

Cabins and camping spaces. Old pecan trees, pool, Jacuzzi, and store. Minutes from downtown. Between I-35N and I-10W. From I-10 exit W.W. White going north. Then left on Gembler.

Creek Hollow RV Park

40970 FM 3159, Canyon Lake 78133
830-899-7121

In the scenic Hill Country with an abundant of wildlife and trees. Golf, boating, rafting, and fishing nearby. Take 281 to 46 going east to 3159 northeast.

Hill Country RV Park

131 Ruekle Road, New Braunfels 78130
830-625-1919

Five minutes from downtown New Braunfels or 30 miles north of San Antonio. Amenities include 300 full hookups and pull: throughs, cable, phones, heated pool, sauna, hot tub, exercise room, and recreation room.

Maricopa Ranch Resort

12915 Hwy 306, Canyon Lake 78132 • 830-964-3731

Convenient to lake and river for tubing, canoeing, fishing, and swimming. Has 140 full hookup sites, cottages with kitchenettes, swimming pool and spa. Take I-35 north and exit 191. Go left 14 miles. Will be on the left.

Locations

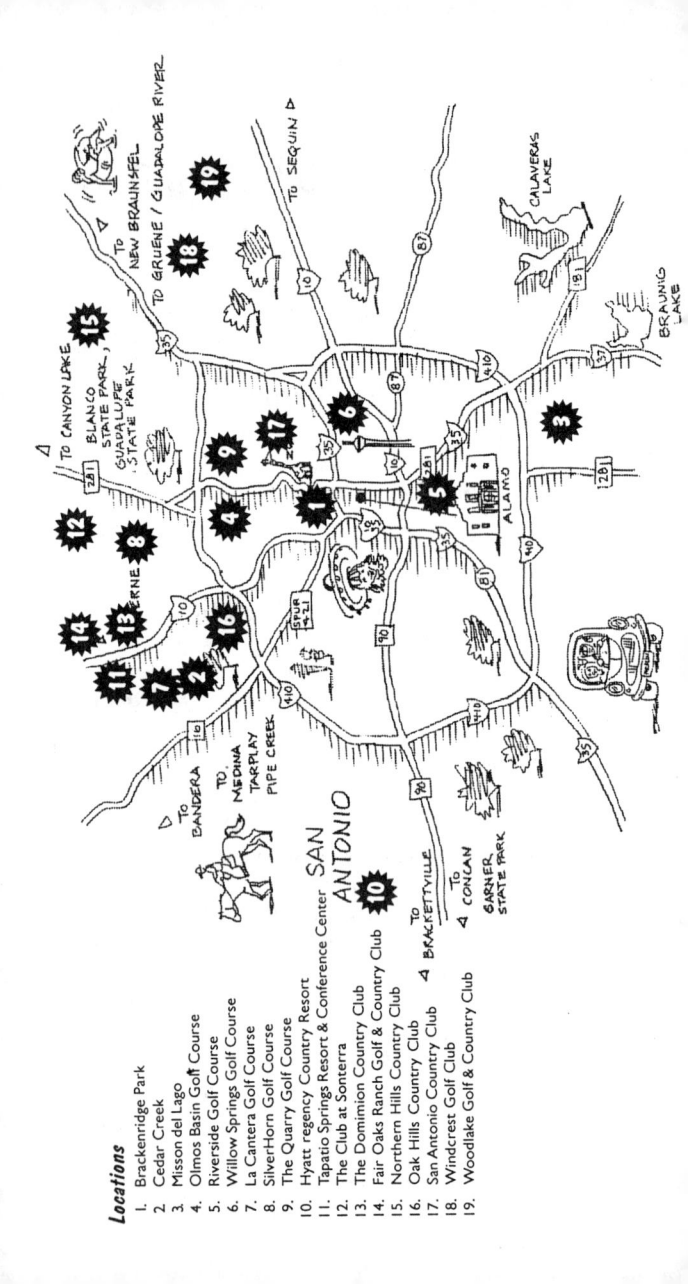

1. Brackenridge Park
2. Cedar Creek
3. Misson del Lago
4. Olmos Basin Golf Course
5. Riverside Golf Course
6. Willow Springs Golf Course
7. La Cantera Golf Course
8. SilverHorn Golf Course
9. The Quarry Golf Course
10. Hyatt regency Country Resort
11. Tapatio Springs Resort & Conference Center
12. The Club at Sonterra
13. The Dominion Country Club
14. Fair Oaks Ranch Golf & Country Club
15. Northern Hills Country Club
16. Oak Hills Country Club
17. San Antonio Country Club
18. Windcrest Golf Club
19. Woodlake Golf & Country Club

Chapter 11
GOLF COURSES IN THE SAN ANTONIO AREA

Municipal Courses
    Brackenridge Park 196
    Cedar Creek 196
    Misson del Lago 196
    Olmos Basin Golf Course 197
    Riverside Golf Course 197
    Willow Springs Golf Course 197

Public and Daily Fee Courses
    La Cantera Golf Course 198
    SilverHorn Golf Course 198
    The Quarry Golf Course 198

Resorts
    Hyatt regency Country Resort 199
    I Tapatio Springs Resort & Conference Center 199

Private Courses
    The Club at Sonterra 199
    The Domimion Country Club 200
    Fair Oaks Ranch Golf & Country Club 200
    Northern Hills Country Club 200
    Oak Hills Country Club 201
    San Antonio Country Club 201
    Windcrest Golf Club 201
    Woodlake Golf & Country Club 201

Golfing in San Antonio

MUNICIPAL COURSES

Brackenridge Park
2315 Avenue B, San Antonio 78218
210-226-5612

Golf at the oldest public course in the state. Designed by the legendary A.W. Tillinghast, this 18-hole hosted the 1st Texas Open in 1922. Having 6185 yards (men) and 5216 (women) the course's front nine is lined with oaks and pecans. Players' tee shots must be accurate to score well. The back nine is open but often windy. Slope 132 Rating 73.4 Par 72. Weekdays $14, weekends $17, cart $18.

Cedar Creek
8050 Vista Colina, San Antonio 78255
210-695-5050

A top-ranking municipal 18-hole course in South Texas. Scenic Cedar Creek's course winds through limestone hillsides taking golfers up and down steep elevations, around several waterfalls and creeks. Different levels of greens make it challenging. With 7158 (men) and 5535 (women), Slope 132, Rating 73.4, Par 72. Weekdays $18, weekends $20, carts $16.

Mission del Lago
1250 Mission Grande, San Antonio 78214
210-627-2522

This 18-hole course is flat, but the Texas wind makes it more challenging. Other difficulties—water on 10 of the holes and subtle greens—test any player's ability, particularly on the back tees. With 7004 yards (men) and 5748 (women), Slope 132, Rating 72.6, Par 72. Weekdays $32, weekends $39. Prices include carts.

Golfing in San Antonio

Olmos Basin Golf Course
7022 N. McCullough, San Antonio 78216
210-826-4041

As one of San Antonio's most popular 18-hole courses, the Olmos Basin Golf Course offers several demanding par 3 holes. The course is fairly straightforward in design—nothing too tricky for a good golfer. With 6894 yards (men) and 5748 (women), Slope 123, Rating 71.0 Par 72.

Riverside Golf Course
203 McDonald, San Antonio 78210
210-533-8371

Teddy Roosevelt and his Rough Riders trained at this site. This 18-hole course offers an all par 3 course, plus a full-size 18-hole championship course (6602 yards men, 5748, women). With trees lining the fairways, it's a straight hitter's advantage. The back nine is for the long hitters. Slope 128, Rating 71.5, Par 72. Weekdays $14, weekends $17, and carts $18.

Willow Springs Golf Course
202 Coliseum Road, San Antonio 78219
210-226-6721

Willow Springs features the longest hole in San Antonio- a 663-yard par-5 second hole. Hosting many Texas Opens with famous players like Ben Hogan and Bryon Nelson, this 18-hole course is noted for challenging par 4s. With 7221 (men) and 5792 (women), Slope 121, Rating 73.9, Par 72. Weekdays $14, weekends $17, and carts $16.

Golfing in San Antonio

PUBLIC AND DAILY FEE COURSES

La Cantera Golf Club

16641 La Cantera Parkway, San Antonio
210 558-4653 • 800-446-5387

Designed by Jay Morrish and Tom Weiskopf, La Cantera rates as the "best public course" in Texas, hosting the Texas Open four years in a row. Golfers tee up and down on a scenic multi-tiered range. An 18-hole course with 7155 yards (men) and 4940 (women), Slope 132 Rating, Par 72. Weekdays $105, Weekends $115.

SilverHorn Golf Club

1100 Bitters Road, San Antonio 78216
210-545-5300

San Antonio's newest course designed by a well-known architect Randy Heckenkemper, with help from PGA tour pros Scott Verplank and Willie Wood. Perhaps San Antonio's finest course, heavily forested with rolling hills, the SilverHorn Golf Club has a 7000-yard layout with 262 acres. Yards: Gold 6922; Black 6336; Silver 5836. Rating Gold 73.1 Black 70.6 Silver 68.2. Fees: $75 includes cart.

The Quarry Golf Club

444 East Basse Road, San Antonio, 78212
210-824-4500

Its back nine sits in an old limestone quarry framed by 100-foot bluffs. Named in Golfweek Magazine as "America's Best—#2" and in Golf Digest as "Best Course—#4 in Texas." Many par 4s are tough. The windy front nine—designed like the British Open links-style courses—challenge any golfer. With 6740

Golfing in San Antonio

RESORTS

Hyatt Regency Hill Country Resort

9800 Hyatt Resort Dr.
San Antonio, 78251
210-647-1234 888-901-4653

Designed by Arthur Hill, this 18-hole course will challenge any player. Scenic with trees and a Hill Country atmosphere. Yards: 6913 men, 4781 women. Slope 114, Rating 67.8, Par 72. Fee: $100—includes cart.

Tapatio Springs Resort & Conference Center

I-10 West to Exit #539
Johns Road, Boerne, TX
210-696-3539 800-999-3299

A spectacular 18-hole Hill Country golf course with splendid views. Will challenge any player, with water on 14 of the holes. Yards: 6500 men, 6200 women. Slope 122, Rating 70.6, Par 72. Weekdays $73, weekends $83, includes cart.

PRIVATE COURSES

The Club at Sonterra

901 Sonterra, San Antonio 78285
210-496-1560

Offers two 18-hole courses. "Sunburst" designed by Robert von Hagge and Bruce Devlin features a modern course with every hole having water, mounding, and waste areas. Yards 7070, Slope 132, Rating 73.7. The other course, "Deer Canyon" has a more traditional layout with 6535 yards, Slope 123, Rating 71.1. Reciprocal and member sponsored play is restricted.

Golfing in San Antonio

The Dominion Country Club

One Dominion Drive, San Antonio 78257
210-698-1146

A beautiful 18-hole course—the Home of the Senior PGA Tour's SBC (Southwestern Bell Corporation) at the Dominion Tournament. Beautiful clubhouse. Bentgrass greens. Yards 6785, Slope 126, Rating 72.2. Golf professional must call on player's behalf.

Fair Oaks Ranch Golf & Country Club

7900 Fair Oaks Parkway, San Antonio 78015
210-981-9604

Offers two 18-hole courses in the scenic Hill Country with Bermuda greens—Blackjack Oak: 7077 yards, Slope 131, Rating 73.5. Live Oak: 6884 yards, Slope 131, Rating 73.1, Par 72. Must be a member's guest or a member on the list of reciprocal clubs to play.

Northern Hills Country Club

13202 Scarsdale, San Antonio 78217
210-655-8026

An 18-hole course designed to favor the player who favors the ball in the front nine and the player who draws it on the back nine. Bermuda greens. With 6472 yards, Slope 118, Rating 68.7, Par 72. Closed Mondays.

Golfing in San Antonio

Oak Hills Country Club
5401 Fredericksburg, San Antonio 78229
210-349-5151

Hosted the PGA Tour's Texas Open from 1961-66 and 1977-94. Offers an 18-hole course with 6650 yards, Slope 128, Rating 71.8, Par 71. Designed by the famous A.W. Tillinghast, the course requires membership in the USGA to play. A challenging but traditional layout.

San Antonio Country Club
4100 New Braunfels Avenue, San Antonio 78209
210-824-8861

An 18-hole course in rolling hills with curving fairways. With 6759 yards, Slope 120, Rating 72,1 Par 72. Closed Mondays.

Windcrest Golf Club
8600 Midcrown Drive, San Antonio 78239
210-655-1421

Offers a 9-hole course with different tees for playing 18-holes in all. With 4760 yards, Slope 104, Rating 63.1, Par 68. Closed Mondays.

Woodlake Golf & Country Club
6500 Woodlake Parkway, San Antonio 78244
210-661-6124

Strength and Strategy are the words used to describe the demands of this 18-hole course. Designed by the well-known Desmond Muirhead. With 6691 yards, Slope 129, Rating 72.5, Par 72. Semi-private. Weekdays $30, weekends $40, including carts.

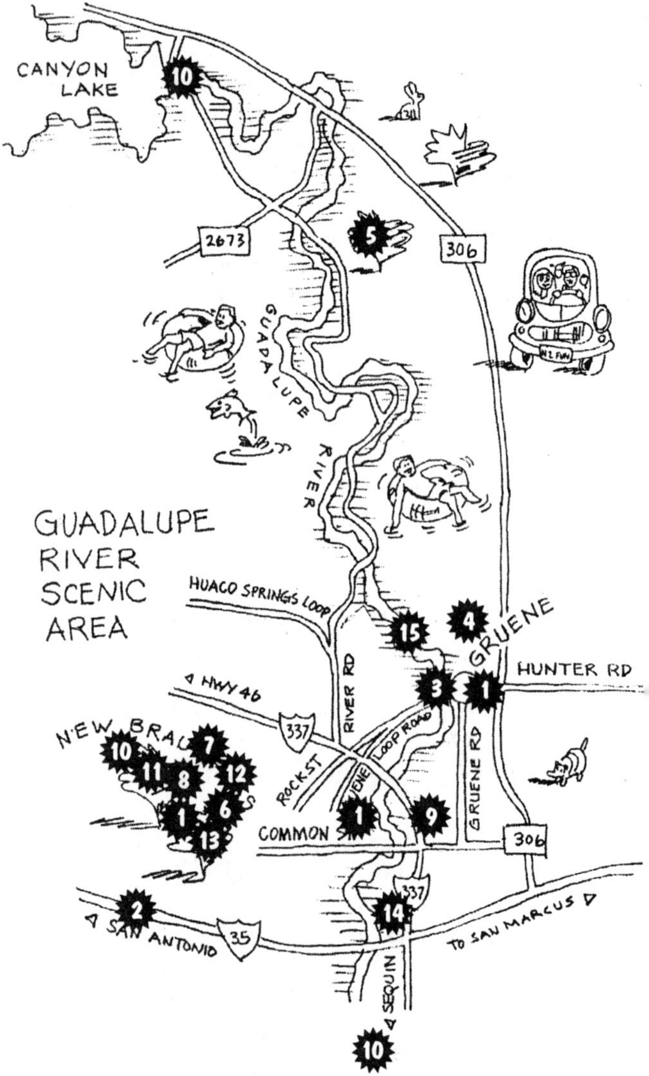
CANYON LAKE
10
2673
5
306
GUADALUPE RIVER
GUADALUPE RIVER SCENIC AREA
HUACO SPRINGS LOOP
RIVER RD
15
4
GRUENE
HUNTER RD
3
1
HWY 46
337
LOOP ROAD
GRUENE RD
NEW BRAUNFELS
10
7
11
8
12
6
1
13
ROCK ST
COMMON ST
1
9
306
2
SAN ANTONIO
35
337
14
TO SAN MARCUS
SEQUIN
10

Chapter 12
NEW BRAUNFELS AND THE GUADALUPE RIVER

1. Antique Shops 204
2. Children's Museum 207
3. Gristmill Restaurant 208
4. Gruene Historic District................. 209
5. Guadalupe River Scenic Area............. 210
6. Hotel Faust............................ 212
7. Hummel Museum 213
8. Landa Park 214
9. Museum of Handmade Furniture.......... 215
10. New Braunfels Golf Courses 216
11. Schlitterbahn Waterpark and Resorts 217
12. Sopheinburg Museum and Archives 219
13. Wurstfest 220
14. The New Braunfels Smokehouse 221
15. The Restaurant at Gruene Mansion 222

New Braunfels And The Guadalupe River

ANTIQUE SHOPS

New Braunfels—known as the "Antique Capital of Texas". Considered world-class shopping for antique lovers. You'll find antique shops well priced. Many locate on San Antonio Street within walking distance of each other. The following are favorites:

Downtowner Antique Mall

223 San Antonio St.
830 629-3947

An antique mall with 15 dealers each with their own specialties. A fun place to browse.

Hours

Daily (Closed Tuesdays.) . . . . 10 am -5 pm
Sundays . . . . 1 am -5 pm

Gruene Antique Co.

1607 Hunter Road
830-629-7781

One of the largest and most well-known places to shop for antiques in the area. The 8000-square-foot store features 28 different collectors and dealers. Offers furniture to small serving items. Located in the Gruene Historic District; housed in the H. B. Gruene's Mercantile Building — a Texas landmark.

Hours

Daily (winter hours) . . . . 10 am - 6 pm
Daily (summer hours) . . . . 10 am - 10 pm

New Braunfels And The Guadalupe River

Headrick Antiques

697 S. Seguin
830-625-1624

Specializing in "real" antiques. Their motto is: "Where browsing is fun and acquiring is exciting." You'll find Early American and Texas Colonial handmade furniture.

Hours

Daily . . . . 10 am - 5 pm
Sundays . . . . 1 pm - 4 pm

New Braunfels And   *The Guadalupe River*

CHILDREN'S MUSEUM

651 Business Loop I-35, Suite 530
New Braunfels 78130
830-620-0939 • 888-928-08326

Children's Museum features New Braunfels' culture

Learn as you play. Reign in a castle (like the one in New Braunfels, Germany). Explore Grandma's attic (Oma's Dachboden), and turn butter or wash with a washboard. Pretend you're a doctor, dress up as a princess or a fireman or a cowboy. Listen to stories and peep through a microscope. The hands-on displaysat the Children's Museum will brighten any child's day.

Annual family memberships offer unlimited admission for very little, $35.

Hours

Mon. – Sat. . . . . 9 am – 5 pm
Sunday . . . . Noon – 5 pm

Cost

Per person $2.50
Members . . . . Free

Directions

From I-35, take exit #188.
Will be in the New Braunfels Marketplace.

New Braunfels And The Guadalupe River

GRISTMILL RIVER RESTAURANT

1287 Gruene Road
Gruene 78130
830-625-0684

A fun place to eat

Dine outdoors in the ruins of an old 1800's cotton gin overlooking the Guadalupe River. Specialties include extra large fries cut in round slices, South Texas polish sausage cooked in barbecue sauce, grilled fillet with cracked black peppers, and marinated grilled chicken breast. Or try their Gristburger with spicy queso sauce. Top this off with their pecan pie or the Hill Country Strawberry Shortcake.

In Gruene, the Gristmill River Restaurant sits directly behind the 100-year old dance hall and under the town's water tower. The restaurant features a retail store with Gristmill hats, mugs, and t-shirts.

Hours

Summer

Daily .... 11 am - 11 pm

Winter

Sun - Thurs. .... 11 am - 10 pm
Fri - Sat .... 11 am - 11 pm

Cost

$3.99 - $13.99

Directions

From I-35, exit 191 and go west 1.5 miles and then left on Hunter Road. Travel .5 miles to Gruene.

New Braunfels And *The Guadalupe River*

GRUENE HISTORIC DISTRICT

Hunters Road, Gruene 78130
830-629-5077

In the 1840's, German farmers settled along the banks of the Guadalupe River, 4 miles out of New Braunfels in Gruene. The first mercantile store opened in 1878, close to the cotton gin along the Guadalupe River. After that came the dance hall and many others during this prosperous time. In the 1920's, the depression and the boll weevil turned the community into a ghost town. Today, the unique buildings of Gruene are listed on the National Register of Historic Places. The town is a thriving tourist attraction.

Places you'll want to see: Gruene General Store, an authentic general store with soda fountain, and BushWhackers, selling fine furniture made from discarded wood pieces. Others favorites include the Lone Star Country Store, Buck Pottery, Cotton-Eyed Joe's, the Gristmill River Restaurant, and the Gruene Mansion Restaurant. Down on the banks of the river, rent tubes and rafts for a float on the Guadalupe River at the Rockin R River Rides, one of the largest river outfits in the area. Rentals include shuttle rides. 830-629-999

The oldest dance hall in Texas, the Gruene Hall, features the best in country, blues, and folk musicians. Many like George Strait, Lyle Lovett, and the Fabulous Thunderbirds have played here.

Hours

(Store hours vary with extended hours in the summer)
Daily . . . . 9 am – 6 pm

Directions

From I-35, take exit 191 (FM 306) west 1.5 miles to Hunter's Road and go left.

New Braunfels And   *The Guadalupe River*

GUADALUPE RIVER SCENIC AREA
canoeing, rafting, tubing

River Road
New Braunfels

The Guadalupe River's a haven for tubers. Drive this scenic River Road, a 15-mile stretch from the city limits of New Braunfels (Loop 337) to Sattler, just below the Canyon Lake Dam. The road meanders along side the Guadalupe River, crossing it four times. Here you'll find one of the most popular spots in Texas for recreation; in fact, 35,000 people tube the river during the Labor Day weekend.

Banks of the river are dotted with outfits that rent tubes, rafts, and canoes, and designated put-ins and take-outs. Tubes rent for $8-9 and include a shuttle ride back. Some tubes come with plastic bottoms for toting smaller kids and ice chests. The Canyon Dam controls water levels; but drought years favor smaller children and flood levels challenge the kayakers. Waters in between please everyone else.

Here is a favorite outfitter and place to stay along the river.

River Valley Resort & Rio Raft Co.

PO Box 2036, Canyon Lake 78130
http://www.new-braunfels.com/rio/
e-mail: rioraft@gvtc.com
830-964-3613   Fax: 830-964-3620

Stay with the nicest folks on the river

Located on a scenic bank of the Guadalupe River with bluffs and huge oaks, pecans, cypress, and junipers, the River Valley Resort offers all the amenities you'll need for a super outing. Rent a tidy cottage: the smallest sleeps 4, the largest 8; park your RV or put up a tent

New Braunfels And The Guadalupe River

along the water's front. Rent a tube or take a raft trip that includes a shuttle ride and life vests.

The convenience store supplies guests with ice, cold drinks, sunscreen, souvenirs, and snacks. This family-oriented resort prides itself on personal service. Popular in the winter with Winter Texans and fly fishermen and in the summer with family reunions. Call ahead 2 or 3 months for reservations.

On the first weekend in October the resort features an authentic Native American Pow Wow. You'll want to attend. Many tribes from around the country—a gathering of nations—celebrate their cultural heritage. Enjoy Indian dancing, arts, crafts, and food booths.

Office hours

Daily .... 9 am – 4 pm

Cost

Tube rental $8-9

Standard Raft Trips

Adults $19
Children under 12 .... $16

Short Raft Trips

Adults $15
Children under 12 .... $12

(Winter rates are lower)

Cabins $75-180
RV Sites $19-23
Camping $18

Directions

From I-35, exit # 191 (FM 306) and travel 13 miles west. Turn left on FM 2673 and go 1½ miles to River Road. Turn left and go 1 mile. Will be on the left.

New Braunfels And   *The Guadalupe River*

HOTEL FAUST

240 South Seguin Street
New Braunfels 78130
830-625-7791

Great old historic hotel in New Braunfels

Old-world charm still abounds at this historic hotel, New Braunfels' oldest. Built in 1929, this distinguished hotel offers guests modern conveniences and affordable rates. Amenities include cable TV, air conditioning, ceiling fans, and telephones. At the same time, you'll enjoy the well-crafted furniture and other 1920's furnishings. Situated between San Antonio and Austin, the hotel offers a great location for recreation in the Hill Country.

Cost

Rooms - Suites: $39 - 135

Directions

From I-35 in new Braunfels, exit on #187. Go west approximately 1 mile. Will be on the left.

New Braunfels And The Guadalupe River

HUMMEL MUSEUM

199 Main Plaza
New Braunfels 78130
800-456-4866

Artwork displays of world-renowned artist

Want a good home for your Hummel figurine? This 15,000-square-foot modern museum accepts donations. Many figurines in their huge collection are valued at thousands of dollars.

As a nun in Germany during World War II, Sister Hummel created her many priceless art pieces, capturing the innocence of humanity. See the largest collection of her original artwork that inspired the Hummel figurines: her charcoals, pastels, oils. To preserve her work, much of it exhibits on a rotating schedule. Next time you come, see more.

Don't miss watching the 45-minute video of Sister Hummel's life. Browse in the gift shop. The tour lasts approximately 2 hours; call for times.

Hours

Mon. – Sat. . . . . 10 am-5 pm

Cost

Adults $5
Students (18-6) $3
Children (under 6) . . . . Free
Seniors $4.50
AAA Members $3

Directions

Located in downtown New Braunfels on the Plaza. Take exit #187 from I-35.

New Braunfels And   *The Guadalupe River*

LANDA PARK

City of New Braunfels Parks and Recreation
110 Golf Course Drive
New Braunfels 78130
830-608-2160

New Braunfels' best-kept secret

This 300-acre park complex, including Prince Solms Park, bursts with things to do. The crystal-clear Comal River, perhaps the shortest river in the world, begins in Landa Park, and flows 2½ miles before emptying into the Guadalupe. Grab your tube for a float or a slide down the Prince Solms Tube Chute. Haven't got a tube? Rent one from the park.

Many of the activities available include an arboretum with 96 species of trees—some over 300 years old, an 18-hole golf course, shaded picnic facilities along the Comal River, an Olympic-size swimming pool, a spring-fed pool, a miniature train, and a miniature golf course. The park rents paddle boats and glass-bottom boats, too. Here's a great place for walking or jogging. Feed the ducks. Go fishing.

Summers include Thursday night concerts in the park.

Hours
Hours for the different attractions vary
Daily . . . . 6 am - midnight

Cost
Varies for the attraction

Directions
From I-35 take exit #187 (Seguin Street) and go north through the city's plaza. Continue on Seguin until you reach Landa Drive and go left. Watch for entrance to the park.

New Braunfels And The Guadalupe River

MUSEUM OF HANDMADE FURNITURE

1370 Church Hill Dr., New Braunfels 78130
830-629-6504

Fine furniture built by German pioneer craftsmen

This unique museum centers on the area's fine pioneer furniture. From as early as 1845, many German immigrant cabinetmakers settled in the Hill Country. Names of these early woodworking settlers include Scholl, Tietze, Jahn, Stautzenberger, and Ebensberger. See original furniture handmade in Texas from the 1860's to the mid-19th century. Housed in the Breustedt Haus, a Texas historic landmark, the museum contains rare and interesting items used in pioneer homes.

The museum includes a log cabin and a one-room cabin furnished with tools and furniture of the early pioneers. Tours are given as visitors come and last an hour. The last tour begins at 3:30 pm.

Hours

Closed Mondays, New Year's, Easter, and after the 1st weekend in Dec.

Jan. - Feb. (Sat. & Sun. only) .... 1 pm - 4 pm
March - May (Wed. – Sun.) ...... 1 pm - 4 pm
June - August
    Tues. - Sat. .... 10 pm - 4 pm
    Sunday .... 1 pm - 4 pm
September - October
    Wed. - Sun. .... 1 pm - 4 pm
November - 1st weekend in December
    Sat. & Sun. only .... 1 pm - 4 pm

Costs

Adults $3
Children (6-12) $1
Children (under 6) Free

Directions

Go I-35N. Exit #189 (Highway 46, Loop 337). Go west. Go through two lights. Go right on Church Hill Road. Will be on the right side.

New Braunfels And The Guadalupe River

NEW BRAUNFELS GOLF COURSES

Golf at one of these courses open to the public. Fees vary according to season. Call for times.

Canyon Lake Golf Course & Country Club

FM 2673 to Startzville, Canyon Lake
830-899-3301

Located 30 minutes from San Antonio. A scenic course with lots of trees and hills that's challenging for the yardage. Semi-private.

Yards: 6016 men, 4726 women.
Slope 122, Rating 68.8, Par 72.
Fees: weekdays $19, weekends $25 including cart.

Landa Park Municipal Golf Course

11445 Agarita Trail, New Braunfels 78130
830-608-2174

One of the busiest courses in Texas. The Landa Park Municipal Golf Course features a traditional wide open, user friendly 18-hole course. The Comal River runs through it.

Yards: 6103 men, 4919 women.
Slope 112, Rating 68.9, Par 72.
Fees: weekdays $12, weekends $15, cart $18.

Long Creek Home of the Bandit

6019 FM 725, McQueeney 78132
830-609-4665

A championship golf course in a beautiful hill country setting. Wide open with 100 foot elevation. Water on 11 of the 18 holes. Challenging. Four sets of tees.

Yards: 6928 men, 5253 women.
Slope 133, Rating 73.6. Par 71.
Fees: weekdays $50, weekends $62, including cart.

New Braunfels And   *The Guadalupe River*

SCHLITTERBAHN WATERPARK AND RESORTS

400 N. Liberty
New Braunfels
830-625-2351

Huge Texas-size water park

See what hi-tech did to a Texas water park. You must ride the Master Blaster, the Schlitterbahn's award-winning, one-of-a-kind uphill water coaster. Fun. Fun. Fun. Of course it's popular - plan to get in line-first thing in the morning.

One of my most favorite places to go, the Schlitterbahn with its German culture and heritage features a 65-acre water park and a resort complex. You'll find over 40 rides and 6 theme areas. Enjoy 3 uphill water coasters—a must-do, 9 tube chutes, 17 water slides, 5 children's water play areas and a tidal wave river. The resort ranges in accommodations from motel rooms, condos, and cottages to furnished homes. Plan ahead to stay here.

This fantastic water park, the largest and most popular in the world, hosts over 800,000 people during their summer season. Peak times for crowds run from July 1 – August 10. Lines get long but the park is extremely well run.

Don't forget to bring a cooler with food for lunch, a tradition at the Schlitterbahn. Grab yourself a table, there are hundreds throughout the park. This is the only large attraction in Texas that allows food and drinks into the park. Or eat lunch at the concessions and restaurants available.

New Braunfels And *The Guadalupe River*

Parking, inner tubes, life vests, and bodyboards are free. Group discounts available as well as season passes. Don't forget the sunscreen.

Hours
Daily ....10 am- 8 pm

All Day Cost *(tax included)*
(Season passe available)

Adults $25.97
Children 3-11 .... $21.64
Children under 3 .... Free

Mid-Day Cost *(after 3:30pm, tax included)*
Adults $18.39
Children 3-11 .... $15.14

Two-Day Cost *(tax included)*
Adults $41.12
Children 3-11 .... $32.46

Directions
From San Antonio, take IH-35 North to New Braunfels. On the north side of New Braunfels take exit 189 and go west on loop 337/Hwy 46. Go left on Common Street.

To main park Castle entrance:
Stay on Common to liberty Street. Go right on Liberty to main entrance on left side of street, Parkin attendants will direct you to the nearest parking lots.

New Braunfels And   *The Guadalupe River*

SOPHEINBURG MUSEUM AND ARCHIVES

401 West Coll Street
New Braunfels 78130
830-629-1572

A history teaching museum

One large trunk weighing no more than 500lbs. came with each German family to settle New Braunfels. Items brought often included the men's work tools that greatly influenced the area. Many families donated these pioneer artifacts to this museum devoted to local family histories. Very interesting, a must-see. The archives at 200 N. Seguin brag of having over a million old photos, old newspapers, oral history accounts, and maps. Their hours are Mon. - Fri., 10 am - 4 pm.

Wander through the museum; plan to spend at least an hour. With ten or more in your group, schedule a tour. Smaller groups may join others.

Hours

Mon. – Sat.	10 am – 5 pm
Sunday	1 pm – 5 pm

Cost

Adults	$1.50
Students under 18	$.50
Children (under 3)	Free
Members	Free

Directions

From San Antonio, take I-35 North and exit Sequin Street. Go left under the freeway towards downtown New Braunfels. Turn left on Coll Street. Go up the hill, will be on the right.

New Braunfels And   *The Guadalupe River*

THE NEW BRAUNFELS SMOKEHOUSE

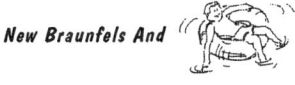

146 Highway 46 E.
New Braunfels 78130
830-625-2416

The New Braunfels Smokehouse, an eating tradition since 1945

A visit to New Braunfels wouldn't be complete without a stop at the New Braunfels Smokehouse. Serving fine home-style breakfasts, lunches, and dinners. During the summer months, enjoy breakfast and barbecue buffets in the Yard. Try their Chicken and Dumplings, one of their specialties, or the Smoked Baby Back Ribs. Don't forget the bread pudding. Before you leave, stock up at their deli with high quality cheeses smoked meats: bacon, jerky, hams, sausages, rib. Better yet, pick up a catalog; they ship anywhere in the U.S.

The delightful decor consists of early Texas antiques. Their gift shop sells gourmet foods, cookbooks, kitchen gifts, handmade items, and more.

Hours

Daily .... 7:30 am – 9 pm

Cost

$5.25-11.95

Directions

At the corner of Highway 46 and I-35. Exit 189.

New Braunfels And — *The Guadalupe River*

THE RESTAURANT AT GRUENE MANSION

1275 Gruene Road
New Braunfels 78131
830-620-0760

Newly opened, the Gruene mansion Restaurant offers fine dining in a beautiful settling. Eat out on the breezy decks facing the Guadalupe River or inside the mansion with the huge rock fireplace. Order one of their fantastic salads. Other exceptional entrees include their Chicken Oporto, the Grilled Salmon, and the New Braunfels Smoked Sausage. They serve tasty pasta dishes and gourmet sandwiches, too. Kids under 10 will enjoy their child's menu. Popular for weddings and catered events. Enjoy live music on Friday and Saturday evenings.

Come during the holidays, when the restaurant is spectacularly decorated in red and gold—it takes them three weeks to put it together.

Hours
Daily .... 11 am – 10 pm

Cost
Lunches $4.95-13.95
Dinner .... $7.95 - 22

Directions
From I-35, take exit 191 (FM 306) west 1.5 miles to Hunter's Road and go left.

New Braunfels And   *The Guadalupe River*

WURSTFEST

178 Landa Park Drive, New Braunfels 78130
830-625-9167 • 800-221-4369

New Braunfels' famous festival

New Braunfels' Wurstfest—a ten-day salute to sausage—rates as "one of the top events in North America." Over 100,000 people attend this festival that begins on the first Friday before the first Monday in November.

Enjoy the best of German food and entertainment: oompah bands, singers, dancers, yodelers, and polkas. Each year, the Wurstfest features a brass band from Germany. Other bands and entertainers like Myron Floren from the Lawrence Welk Show come from around the country to perform each year. With over 40 food booths, eats at the festival includes imported wursts, sausages on a stick, turkey legs, sauerkrauts, potato pancakes, and more.

The festival features arts and crafts and a carnival area for small children. Discounts are available for tickets bought in advance. Ask about group rates.

Hours

Mon.–Wed.	5 pm – 11 pm
Thurs. and Fri.	5 pm – Midnight
Saturdays	11 am – 12:30 am
Sundays	11 am – 10:30 pm
Cost for Adults	$6
Children under 12	Free

Directions

The festival takes place inside Landa Park. Take I-35 North and exit Walnut. Go left for two miles until Walnut intersects with Landa Street. Go right two blocks to the entrance of Landa Park. The festival will be on the left, shortly after entering the park.

INDEX

Index

Symbols

42nd Street 90

A

A Night in Old Vienna 93
Abundare River Ranch 30
Acadiana Cafe 136
Adam's Mark Hotel
 RiverWalk 27, 182
Admiralty Park 193
Air Force History and Traditions
 Museum 62
Aladdin 96
Alamo 10
Alamo Cafe 137
Alamo City Grand Tour 120
Alamo Heights 170
Alamo Pedicab Company 115
Alamo Street Restaurant and
 Theatre 82
Alamo Village 114
Alamo Visitor Center 133
Alamodome 12
Annual Jazz'SAlive 177
Antique Center 164
Antique Shops 164, 204
Apple Annie's Tea Room
 & Bakery 138
Apple Crunch Cake 138
Armstrong Laboratory 100
Armstrong, Louie 87
Arneson River Theatre 83, 119
Arquitectos, Legorreta 18
Art Galleries 165
Artisan's Alley 138
Arts! San Antonio 84
Asian art 74
Austin, Stephen F. 72
Aztec 70

B

Bald Eagle Ranch 30
Ballet San Antonio 85
Bandera Dude and
 Guest Ranches 30
Bandolero 114
Bed and Breakfast Inns 189
Bernhardt, Sarah 183
Big Country River Festival 178
Blanco State Park 34
Blue Star Arts Complex 86
Booksmiths of San Antonio 166
Bookstores 166
Boudro's, A Texas Bistro 139
Bowie, Jim 10, 21
Brackenridge Park 35, 132, 196
Braunig Lake Park 36
Breustedt Haus 214
Brooks Air Force Base 66
Brooks School of Aerospace
 Medicine 100
Buck Pottery 208
Buckhorn Saloon and Museum 63
BushWhackers 208
Bussey's Flea Market 168

C

Calaveras Lake Park 37
Camberley Gunter Hotel 183
Canyon Lake 38
Canyon Lake Golf Course &
 Country Club 215
Carranza's 140
Cartier 184
Carver Community Cultural
 Center 87
Casa Navarro State
 Historical Park 39
Cascade Caverns 40
Cave-Without-A-Name 41
Cedar Creek Golf Course 196
Center for Antiques 164

Index

Central Market 167
Cezanne 71
Cheever Books 166
Children's Museum 73, 206
Chinese art 74
Chinese Sunken Garden 121
Chris Madrid's Nachos
    and Burgers 141
Christmas Lighting
    Ceremony 17, 178
Chukka Creek Guest Ranch 30
Cider Mill 104
CinFestival 88
Class Pass 133
Club at Sonterra 199
Comal River 213, 215
Copper Kitchen Restaurant 97
Cotton-Eyed Joe's, 208
Count Basie 87
Cowboy Capital of the World 30
Crazy for You 90
Creek Hollow RV Park 193
Crockett, Davy 10, 21, 24
Crockett Hotel 185
Crown Plaza St. Anthony 184
Crystal Ice Palace 116

D

Daddy's Dying, Who's Got the Will 94
Dagen Bela Ortiz Galeria 165
Days Inn and Suites Fiesta Park 192
Deer Canyon Golf Course 199
Desert Storm 78
Devlin, Bruce 199
DeYoung 184
Dick's Last Resort 142
Discovery Zone 117
Dixie Dude Ranch 31
Dixie Kampground 193
Dominion Country Club 200
Driving Miss Daisy 96

E

Ebensberger 214
Eberson, John 92
Edward H. White Museum 66
Eisenhauer Road Flea Market 168
Eisenhower Park 42
El Mirador Restaurant 143
Ellington, Duke 87
Embassy Skate Center 118
Emily Edwards Gallery 97
Espada Acequia and Aqueduct 64
Espada Dam 64
Experience Austin 120

F

Fabulous Thunderbirds 208
Faces and Places of Texas 68
Fair Oaks Ranch Golf & Country
    Club 200
Fairfield Inn by Marriott 192
Fairmount Hotel 182
Fandangos 186
Farm Country Club 33
Farm to Market 167
Farmers Market Plaza 15
Feria de Santa Cecilia & Fiestas
    Navidenas 179
Fiesta Art Fair 97
Fiesta Celebration 14
Fiesta Competition 116
Fiesta de las Luminarias 179
Fiesta River Parade 17
Fiestas Patrias 177
Fitzgerald, Ella 87
Flea Markets 168
Flying L Guest Ranch 31
Food Markets 167
Fort Sam Houston 132
Fort Sam Houston Museum 65
Friedrich, Albert 63
Friedrich Wilderness Park 42, 43
Furniture and Antique Consign-
    ment Shop 204

Index

G

Gallery of the Southwest 165
Gauguin 71
Geronimo 65
Ghost Hunt 13
Ghost investigator 13
Gillespie, Dizzy 87
Glenn, John 100
Golden Wok Chinese Restaurant 144
Goodwill Industries 102
Grand Virage 126
Grant, Ulysses S. 183
Grayline of San Antonio Lone Star Trolley Tour 119
GrayLine Tours of San Antonio 120
Great Hill Country Pumpkin Patch 104
Grey Moss Inn 146
Gristburger 207
Gristmill River Restaurant 207
Gruene Antique Co. 204
Gruene General Store 208
Gruene Hall 208
Gruene Historic District 208
Guadalupe Cultural Arts Center 88
Guadalupe River Scenic Area 209
Gully Washer 23
Gunther House Rest. 14, 145

H

H.E.B. Science Treehouse 26, 73
Hall of Feathers 63
Hall of Fins 63
Hall of Horns 63
Hall of Texas History 63
Hampton Inn Sea World 192
Handel's Messiah 93
Hanger 9 66
Hansel and Gretel 93
Hard Rock Café 147
Harlequin Dinner Theater 89
Haunted Places Tours 13
Headrick Antiques 205
Heard Ranch Roundup 101
Heckenkemper, Randy 198
Henry B. Gonzales Convention Center 17
Hertzberg Circus Museum 67
Hill Country RV Park 193
Hilton Palacio del Rio 184
Historic Camberley Gunter Hotel 183
Historic Crown Plaza St. Anthony 184
Historic King Williams District Walking Tou 14
Historic Menger Hotel 183
Hogan, Ben 197
Holiday Inn Crockett Hotel 185
Holiday Inn Express Hotel & Suites 192
Holiday Inn River Walk 186
Holiday River Parade 17
Homewood Suites River Walk 186
Hopi Indians 165
Hotel Faust 211
Human Systems Center 100
Hummel Museum 212
Humpty-Dumpty's Pumpkin Patch 96
Hyatt Regency Hill Country Resort 187, 199

I

I Hate Hamlet 89
IMAX Theater 11
Institute of Texan Cultures 68, 119
Instrument Petting Zoo 93
Inter-American Bookfair and Literary Festival 88, 178

Index

Interactive Classics 93
International Ghost Hunters
    Society 13
Irish elk antlers 63

J

Jackson House, Noble Inn 190
Jahn 214
Japanese Tea Garden 35, 121
John Wayne Museum 114
Joker's Revenge 23
Josephine Theater 90
Jungle Jim's Playland 122

K

Kallison's Western Wear 171
Kiddie Park 123
Kids' Kove 131
King Ferdinand III 21
King Phillip V 21
King Williams Fair 14
King Williams Historic District 17

L

La Cantera Golf Club 198
La Fogata 148
La Mansion del Rio Hotel
    179, 187
La Margarita Mexican Restaurant
    15
La Villita 119, 132
La Villita Historic District 69, 170
Lackland Air Force Base 62
Landa Park 213
Landa Park Municipal Golf Course
    215
Landing 27
Las Posadas 179
Laser Quest 124
Latin American Art 74

LBJ Homesites 120
Lee, Robert E. 183
LH7 Ranch Resort 32
Liberty Bar 149
Lighting Ceremony 178
Lightning Ranch 32, 103
Little Shop of Horrors 94
Lone Star Brewery 74
Lone Star Buckhorn
    Museum 63, 119, 132
Lone Star Country Store 208
Lone Star Luge 131
Lone Star Trolley Tour 119
Lonesome Dove 114
Long Barracks Museum 10
Long Creek Home
    of the Bandit 215
Love Creek Orchards, Nature, and
    Birding Tours 104
Lovett, Lyle 208
Lucchese Boots 171

M

Madonna 129
Magic Time Machine 150
Magik Children's Theater 91
Majestic Performing
    Arts Center 92
Majestic Theater 84
Malibu Castle and Malibu Grand
    Prix 126
Man of La Mancha 94
Maricopa Ranch Resort 193
Market Square
    15, 95, 119, 132, 170
Marriot 27
Marriott Riverwalk/Rivercenter
    188
Match Makers 96
Matisse 71
Mayan Ranch 32

Index

McNay Art Museum 71, 132
McNay, Marion Koogler 71
Menger Hotel 183
Mexican Cultural Institute 70
Mexican folk art 86, 165
Mi Tierra Café 15, 95, 151
Milam Park 95
Mini Virage 126
Mission Concepcion 119, 132
Mission del Lago Golf Course 196
Mission Espada 64
Mission San Jose 19, 119, 132
Mission Trail 64, 120
Mission Trails Bike Rentals 127
Morrish, Jay 198
Mud Festival 17
Muirhead, Desmond 201
Museum of Handmade
  Furniture 214
My Fair Lady 90

N

Native American Pow Wow 210
Navaho 165
Navarro, Don Jose Antonio 39
Nelson A. Rockefeller Center for
  Latin American Art 74
Nelson, Bryan 197
New Braunfels Golf Courses 215
New Braunfels Smokehouse 219
Night in Old San Antonio 69
Noble Inns 190
Northern Hills Country Club 200

O

Oak Hills Country Club 201
Odd Couple—a female version 96
Oge Carriage House 79
Oge House Inn 191
Oge, Louis 191
O'Keefe 71

Oktoberfest San Antonio 178
Old San Francisco Steakhouse 152
Olmos Basin Golf Course 197
Olmos Park 132
Oma's Dachboden 206
Outlet Stores 169

P

Paloma Blanca 153
Pancoast Carriage House, Noble
  Inn 190
Pape's Pecan House 106
Paris Hatter 171
Passenger Pigeons 63
Passion Play 21
Pearl Harbor 121
Picasso 71
Pioneer Mills 14, 145
Pioneer, Trail Drivers and Texas
  Ranger Memorial M 72
Planet Hollywood 154
Plaza San Antonio 188
Pollack 71
Pope John Paul II 21
Postert House 79
Pre-Columbian gallery 74
Promised Land Barnyard 107

Q

Quadrangle, The 65
Quarry Golf Club 198
Quarry Market East 170

R

Radisson Market Square 192
Ramblin' River 187
Rattler 23
Remington 184
Residence Inn Alamo Plaza 192
Restaurant at Gruene Mansion
  220

Index

Retama Park 128
Return of the Chili Queens 176
Revolutionary War 78
Rio Rio Cantina 155
Ripley's Believe It or Not Plaza Theatre of Wax 129
River Valley Resorts & Rio Raft Co. 209
River Walk 17, 27
River Walk Holiday Parade 178
Rivercenter Christmas Pageant 179
Rivercenter Mall 16
RiverDance 84
Riverside Golf Course 197
Riverwalk Inn Bed and Breakfast 189
Rockin R River Rides 208
Roosevelt, Teddy 197
Rough Riders 197
Rudy's Country Store and BBQ 156
Running R Ranch 33
RV Parks and Camping 193

S

San Angel Folk Art, Inc. 86
San Antonio Botanical Gardens 84, 132
San Antonio Central Library 18
San Antonio Conservation Society 17, 69, 79
San Antonio Conservation Society Office 14
San Antonio Country Club 201
San Antonio LightHouse 109
San Antonio Mission National Historic Park 19
San Antonio Museum of Art 74, 132
San Antonio Parks Foundation 177
San Antonio Sampler 120
San Antonio Streetcars 133
San Antonio Symphony 93
San Antonio Zoological Gardens & Aquariums 20
San Antonio's Children's Museum 73
San Antonio's Little Village 69
San Fernando Cathedral 21, 119, 132
San Pedro Playhouse 94
Santa Rosa Children's Hospital 95
SAS Factory Shoe Store 169
Sawdust Pie 138
Schilo's Delicatessen 157
Schlitterbahn Waterpark and Resorts 216
Scholl 214
Scobee Planetarium 130
Sea Island Shrimp House 158
Seaworld of Texas 22
Shakespeare in the Park 84, 176
Sheraton 27
Show Place Hills 108
Silver Spur Dude Ranch 33
SilverHorn Golf Club 198
Sister Hummel 212
Six Flags Fiesta Texas 23
Snow White and the Seven Dwarfs 94
Social Security 96
Sopheinburg Museum 218
Southwest School of Arts and Crafts 97
Spanish Governor's Palace, 75, 119
Spirit of Healing 95
Spirits of San Antonio Tour 110
Splashtown 131
Spurs 12
SR-71 Blackbird 62
Stautzenberger 214
Steven Stoli Playhouse and The Backyard Theater 96
Steves Homestead 76

Index

Strait, George 208
Streetcar Pass 133
Streets of Laredo 114
Studebaker Carriage 77
Sunburst Golf Course 199
Super 8 Motel Six Flags Fiesta Texas 192

T

Tales of Two Cities 120
Tanger Outlet Center 169
Tapatio Springs Resort & Conference Center 199
Teddy Bear Hospital 73
Tejano Conjunto Festival 88
Texas Adventure Theater 24
Texas Folklife Festival 177
Texas Hill Country Escape 120
Texas Ranger Louis Oge 191
Texas Rangers 72
Texas Trails Gallery 165
Texas Transportation Museum 77
Texas Trolley Hop 132
The City Mouse and The Country Mouse 96
The Club at Sonterra 199
The Dominion Country Club 200
The Grinch 91
The King and I 94
The Man Who Came to Dinner 89
The Nutcracker 84, 85, 93
The Phantom of the Alamo 91
The Quarry Golf Club 198
The St. Anthony 184
The Stamping Factory 138
The Tale of a Fourth Grade Nothing 91
The Three Pigs 96
Thumb, Tom 67
Tietze 214
Tillinghast, A.W. 196, 201
Toulouse-Lautrec 71
Tower of the Americas 25, 119, 159
Travis, Col. William 10, 21
Travis Park 184
Treviño, Jesse 95
True Women Tours 111
Turkey in the Store 96
Twig Bookshop 166
Twin Elm Guest Ranch 32

U

U.S Army Medical Department Museum 78
Unique Places To Shop 170
Unique Shops 171
Upper Guadalupe River 38
Ursuline Academy 97
Ursuline Gallery 97

V

Van Gogh 71
Van Halen's guitar 147
VIA Metropolitan Transit 133
VIA San Antonio Streetcars 133
VIA's Class Pass 133
Victorian Brougham Carriage 77
Vietnam 62
Villa de San Fernando 21
Virage 126
Von Hagge, Robert 199

W

Wait 'til Dark 89
War of the Worlds 96
Watching for MacArthur 96
Wax museum 63
Wayne, John 114
Weiskopf, Tom 198
Wilde, Oscar 183
Williams, Docia 110
Willow Springs Golf Course 197

Index

Windcrest Golf Club 201
Witte Museum 26, 132
Woodlake Golf & Country Club 201
World War I 62
World War II 62, 78, 212
Wurstfest 221

Y

Yanaguana River Cruise 27, 119
Yellow Rose Ranch 31
Yturri-Edmunds Historic Site 64, 79

Z

Zuni Indians 165
Zuni Grill 160

Copy and mail this form with your check to:
Into Fun, Company Publications
Order Form
P.O. Box 2494, Sugar Land, Texas 77487-2494
281-980-9745 • Fax: 281-494-9745

Cost per T-shirt: $12.95

Call for information on purchasing INTO FUN T-shirts.

$ Many of the San Antonio establishments offer discounts for any purchaser of *122 Fun Things to do in San Antonio*. Please call 281-980-9745 to find out what savings are available.

Please send me the following:
Total # Books____ @$12.95 each = $____
Shipping, Handling: $4.25 + 8.25% sales tax = $____
Total included .. $____

Send to:

Name _____

Company Name _____

Mailing address _____
_____

City/ State/ Zip _____
_____

Phone _____